MOSTLY TRUE

Stories with a *Southern* Sensibility

Mostly True
Janie Dempsey Watts
Bold Horses Press, Ringgold, Georgia
1. Southern Storytelling 2. Anthologies—Literary Nonfiction 3. Janie Dempsey Watts—Nonfiction 4. Southern Memoir 5. Rural Life Essays 6. Short Stories—Nonfiction 7. Country Living

First edition: October 2025

Cover design by Amber Lanier Nagle

Print ISBN: 979-8-218-83846-1
Library of Congress Control Number: 2026901225

Printed in the United States of America

MOSTLY TRUE

Stories with a *Southern* Sensibility

by

Janie Dempsey Watts

DEDICATION

This book is dedicated to the people of the valley and to storytellers everywhere.

CONTENTS

INTRODUCTION

This is a collection of short creative non-fiction stories. What is a creative non-fiction story anyway? Imagine a tasty dish of plain, vanilla ice cream. That's non-fiction. Then, add chocolate syrup, nuts, and whipped cream. Plop a cherry on top. A huge scarlet red cherry, about the size of a baseball. That's creative non-fiction.

I wrote these stories in the early 2000s all the way to the present. Some were originally published in *Chicken Soup for the Soul* books, and others were published in my "Boomerang" column for *Catoosa Life Magazine* over a nine-year span. A few appeared in other magazines, some were in newspapers, and a few were published in anthologies. Several stories in this book are new, never-before-published pieces. They are set in a variety of places, North Georgia, California, Pennsylvania, and Europe, and different time periods, from my youth all the way to the present day.

Not only did I want to have my stories in one book, but I also wanted to share them with readers who have not had the opportunity to delve into creative non-fiction. I hope you enjoy reading them as much as I have enjoyed creating them.

A LEGACY OF TELLING STORIES

Georgia, 1950s-1960s

Like most Southerners, my daddy's family loved to talk and tell stories. Often, it would be over supper at Grandma's table, covered with oilcloth and plates of leftovers from Sunday dinner at her house nestled in the valley alongside Taylor's Ridge in Ringgold.

Grandma's "leftovers" were a feast—fresh sliced tomatoes from her garden, pickled beets, green beans cooked long and slow until they were tender, pan-fried okra, and cornbread served with soft butter. Of course there was iced tea, and for dessert, sliced pound cake.

The real treat was the conversation that took place around the table after the meal. The stories usually began with one of the children asking Grandma Watts a question about the "olden" days.

"Tell us the story about your grandma and the Civil War," a cousin would say. Grandma would explain how the Gatewood Scouts had tried to take her grandmother's beloved mare named Snip. Grandma Seabolt jumped on the horse and refused to get off. She accompanied the Scouts all the way to Calhoun before they gave up on stealing that mare.

On days when it was too hot to ride our horses, I'd join Grandma on her cool porch with a rocking-chair view of Taylor's Ridge. "Grandma, can you tell me about your grandma and the Cherokee?" Grandma would nod and launch into the story of her great-grandmother, who had lived in the Woodstation Valley alongside the Cherokee back in the 1800s.

"Just down there," she'd say, pointing south, "where Temperance Hall Road meets the highway, they used to gather. One time my great-grandma came up on one of their celebrations. They had a big, old pot of stew cooking over the fire made from a whole skinned rabbit, deer meat, squirrel, squash, and roasting ears. Conahaney stew, I believe she said it was called."

"The whole rabbit?" I asked. "Yes, except for the skin," she said. "The Cherokee invited her to stay and eat with them."

“Did she?” I asked.

Grandma shook her head no. “She’d seen them toss in that whole rabbit.”

As Grandma talked, I could see the Cherokee people dancing while that hot, bubbly stew boiled in a pot over the fire. I could see that shy girl come onto the scene, and the Cherokee motioning for her to come over and join them.

Grandma knew how to tell a story, just as her grandma had told stories to her. Although my great-great-great grandmother never tried that stew, the story lives on.

Another family tale revolved around Grandma’s Williams ancestor, a blacksmith who smelted silver brought to him by the Cherokee who rode over Taylor’s Ridge bearing lumps of silver in their saddlebags. Their secret silver mine has never been found. I found this family story so intriguing that I explored it further and used it as a plot of my first novel *Moon Over Taylor’s Ridge.*

Other families may pass down heirlooms like antiques or family china. Mine passed down the gift of storytelling, a legacy I will always treasure.

BORN A HORSE LOVER

Georgia, 1950s-1960s

I have always loved horses. Before we had them, I remember trying to talk my father into letting me ride a cow. I don't think he did, but when I was seven, he drove up and unloaded a pony during my birthday party. Tommy was a black and white Shetland so gentle you could lie down on the ground under his belly although I'm not sure why anyone would want to. I also jumped up on his back from behind, rode him backward and taught him to jump low walls and climb stairs. Although Tommy didn't know it, he was going to be a circus pony, at least in my mind. He never made it to the big top, but his tender and patient spirit helped build my confidence and taught me trust. After a few years of hearing me talk about palominos, Daddy traded Tommy for a feisty little golden pony with flaxen mane and tail. I couldn't believe I finally owned such a lovely creature. The first time I walked behind her, she kicked me in the stomach, and I fell to the ground in a breathless heap. For the next year, I tried to train her, but she was ornery and just plain mean. I got what I deserved, trading in the familiar and reliability for the flashy. "Beware of what you wish for" now made sense.

Soon, our herd expanded as Daddy bought more ponies and horses to populate our pastures. Our prissy Welsh pony, Flicka, looked delicate and refined, but she seemed to be on a suicide mission when someone climbed aboard. She would take the bit in her mouth and run for the nearest barbed wire fence. Although one of the most beautiful of our herd, she was unpredictable. From her, I learned that beauty can be dangerous.

A small, part-Quarter Horse filly, Peanut, took me into my adolescence. With her scooped nose, her face almost looked Arabian although most folks who looked at her simply called her plump. Since I had no formal training, and a desire to show her in the pleasure class one summer, I asked Dad for riding lessons. He promptly answered, "No, Ma'am. There's nothing they can teach you. You already know how to ride." That summer, Mama took me to every horse show within driving distance, so I could observe the horses and riders in the ring. I also watched my best friend, Ellen, as she took riding lessons. I spent long, hot days training Peanut in the big field in front of Grandma's house. By summer's end, Peanut seemed show-worthy, and I had learned another lesson: self-reliance.

A few years later, I fell for a spirited (wild, actually) part-Arabian stallion. Like many bad boys, Sunny came with a reputation. No one had yet tamed him, and that was my challenge. I spent hours working with Sunny trying to stop him from rearing up. Once he got his front legs up in the air, he just kept going up and sometimes over, till he fell back on top of his rider, which is what happened to me once. Shaken up, but not seriously injured, I vowed to always either use a martingale or never let him get his head up too high when I was aboard.

One summer, my uncle arranged for Sunny and me to be the flag bearers during the opening of a nearby horse show. Carrying the American flag in one hand and keeping Sunny in check with the other was an awkward exercise, especially when Sunny got a whiff of nearby mares. I managed to keep him under control until the invocation when he reared straight up. Thankfully, since everyone was supposed to have their eyes closed in prayer, not too many witnessed this stunt. He came back down just as the prayer was done, and we galloped out of the ring, displaying the fluttering flag to loud applause. That day, Sunny taught me about grace under pressure.

Over the years, when I was growing up, we had more than 40 horses come and go in our herd. Each had a unique personality, and many I could call friends. I can't recall all their names, but I like to remember them as my "gift horses" for all the valuable lessons they shared. If you are lucky enough to have a "gift horse" in your life, throw your arms around his neck and give him a big hug. And if you must, go ahead and look him in the mouth. Just be careful not to get nipped!

TENDING OKRA

Georgia, 1950s

The summer I was eight, Mama faced a serious illness and was hospitalized for several months. I missed her terribly and wondered if she would ever get well enough to come home. In her absence, my father sent me out to stay at our family's farm with aunts and uncles and sometimes with my grandmother. An energetic and vital 74, Grandma tried her best to keep me busy.

One humid Georgia afternoon she took me into her garden to pick okra. She crouched over the plants with her paring knife, cutting off the prickly-haired pods while I watched, wiggling my bare toes in the soft, damp mound of red dirt that ran between the rows. She wore one of her faded cotton bonnets, a pink and white flowered number with a bow firmly tied under chin.

"Why do you wear that bonnet?" I asked.

"To keep my head cool," she answered as she continued cutting off the okra. When the silver bucket I held was about half full, Grandma stood up and wiped her hands on her flour-sack cloth apron. She glanced down at the bucket and said, "I'd say that's a mess of okra, wouldn't you?"

"Yes, ma'am," I answered. "How much is a mess?" She laughed.

"Enough to feed a mess of people," she said, and we headed back inside the cool kitchen with the window that overlooked her garden. I sat in the chair by the family-sized round table that took up most of the kitchen, watching Grandma carefully rinse off okra, cut off stems, and slice pods into pinwheels. The okra looked so slimy, but it didn't bother me. I knew that the gooey pods would turn into crunchy brown morsels after Grandma worked her magic. Carrying the big bowl of sliced okra in her hands, she walked across the kitchen to a special drawer, or bin, where she kept her cornmeal and flour. She reached in, scooped up a few handfuls of cornmeal and flour, and tossed them atop the okra. She added a little salt and pepper, then gave me a spoon to stir the okra until it was coated with powdery ingredients. She heated bacon drippings in a large, black cast-iron skillet.

When the oil started smoking, she tossed in the okra and started the long frying process, which could take up to an hour.

"You have to tend to your okra," she said. "So it gets nice and brown and crispy. Okra needs lots of attention," she said and smiled at me. While she tended the okra, we talked about okra and everything else. Grandma explained that the smaller pods were the best, while the bigger pods were tough and stringy and often dried out. Then she'd move on to other subjects such as the hard days when she and her family ran a dairy farm, and she cooked for the hired hands and her family of eight. She told me about *her* grandma standing up to some scouts who'd tried to take her favorite mare during the Civil War. As she patiently cooked the okra, I listened to her stories which always ended with our family triumphing over some problem or misfortune. Her tales made me feel safe and secure. Hearing that our family had survived so many difficulties, I began to believe that my mother might one day get well and be able to come home.

After what seemed like an eternity of cooking, Grandma would ask me to put out forks, napkins, and a trivet. As she set the hot skillet down on the trivet, I smelled the fragrant steam rising off the hot okra and sat down at my place, so she could serve me a generous portion.

"Okra sure takes a lot of tending," I said.

"You're worth it," she said as I took my first bite, letting the crispy bits sizzle against my tongue.

These days when I feel like I need a little nurturing, I'll cook up a batch of okra and think of those special times with my grandmother. I now realize that Grandma wasn't really just tending to the okra, she was also tending to my spirit.

Newfangled Version of Grandma Watts' Fried Okra

(serves 4 people, or 3 really hungry folks)

1 lb fresh okra or 1 lb frozen okra, thawed

½ cup corn muffin mix

2 tablespoons olive oil

Dash of cayenne pepper

Salt and pepper to taste

Wash okra and cut off hard stem area. Slice remaining pods into pinwheels. Toss in muffin mix, coating well. Heat oil in a large, non-stick skillet. Toss okra into pan, stirring as needed.

Tend okra until crispy and browned. Drain on paper towels and serve up hot.

FALL RITUAL IN NORTHWEST GEORGIA

Georgia, 1950s-1960s

The hype began in late summer as days grew longer and hotter, and tedium had set in, along with horse flies as large as hummingbirds. Fathers and uncles began talking it up, always just in earshot of the younger children who had never taken the journey up the side of long, low-slung Taylor's Ridge in Northwest Georgia. Phrases such as "you'll have to find the right size bag to catch it" and "darned thing almost tore my head off" were tossed around as suspense built. Older children who had experienced the journey wouldn't divulge the details, except to say the creatures were scarier than possums and that the hike into the woods was a long one, lasting into the night when bats came out.

The fall ritual called "The Snipe Hunt" was more mysterious than Halloween and had an edge of danger. For children of Taylor's Ridge Valley brought up in the second half of the 20th century, the snipe hunt was a rite of passage. Although some teens occasionally ventured into the forest in small groups with no adults, the usual participants were younger and were led on the snipe hunting expedition by a band of older family members. In our family, children of a certain age, too old for diapers, young enough to believe in Santa Claus and the tooth fairy, were allowed to participate.

The ideal time for a snipe hunt was somewhere after the harvest but before Halloween and hog-killing weather, when leaves crackled underfoot and the chill had set in for the night. It was usually late on a Sunday afternoon when snipe hunters, large and small, pulled on long overalls and jeans, gathered up large, brown paper bags, lanterns, and jugs of water, and started up the side of Taylor's Ridge. A favorite uncle led the procession into the deep woods, his footsteps muffled by a bed of pine needles.

Suddenly, his hand went up, signaling all to stop. "Listen. Can you hear it?" he whispered. The snipe hunters peered through the thick branches of the evergreens, searching for a pair of glowing eyes, or worse yet, feral teeth. Suddenly one of the fathers would whoop like a native. Propelled by the twin emotions of excitement and fear, the children scattered out into the woods behind the men like a flock of frightened chickens. More often than not, adults became separated from children, and fears were heightened. Trees seemed to grow taller, more menacing, with no adult in charge.

"Where are you, Daddy?" A child called, but the only response was silence. The children slowed down their paces and listened, not only for adults, but also for the snipes, which were said to be quite dangerous if approached the wrong way. Suddenly a twig snapped, and a birdcall sound penetrated the quietness.

"Whoo, whoo," came from somewhere just ahead in the dense forest. The children stopped, huddled together in fear, and listened. They saw a flash of color.

"Is that the snipe?" one whispered, and "Should we go that a way?" and "Will it bite us?" Curiosity was stronger than danger as they proceeded carefully toward the source of the "whoo, whoo" noise. Suddenly a father jumped and screamed "boo," and the children all laughed in relief. Inevitably, one asked, "Did you see the snipe?" Then, the father held his hands about a foot apart and described the elusive snipe, which had the sharpest teeth he'd ever seen.

The snipe hunt went on in this manner for several hours, even into the deep darkness when the cold crept in, and the children's cheeks grew pink and numb. The continued bursts of adrenaline being released into young bodies finally gave way to exhaustion, and one of the band suggested getting off the mountain before the blackness made it impossible to see.

As the parade of tired adults and children straggled back down through the woods, the lantern's glow fading, the adults continued to boast of the snipe they'd seen. The children were left with hope for better luck on snipe hunts yet to come.

By the following summer, when it was time to recruit a new crop of children for the fall ritual, veteran snipe hunters were the first to start the hype. When an older child found himself boasting to a younger cousin about the snipe that got away, found he enjoyed watching the little ones anticipate the snipe hunt, he had truly made the journey, not only up the side of Taylor's Ridge, but to his older, wiser self.

FROSTY GEORGIA MORNING

Georgia, 1960s

On a frosty Georgia morning, in our old Ford truck, Dad and I drove down the dirt road to the barn on the way to check on our horses. We made an odd, silent pair. I was an awkward 12-year-old on the brink of womanhood, suspended in the ugly duckling stage. Dad seemed to have pulled back lately, and I was unsure of his love, now that I was no longer little or cute. One thing was certain, though, we both shared a passion for our horses.

A cold snap had swept into the Valley overnight. My favorite of our seven horses, Peanut, had given birth to her first colt the day before, and although we had seen the foal right after she delivered, I was anxious to get back down to the farm, run my hands through the colt's thick chocolate coat, softer than a stuffed animal.

We were excited about this colt, the son of Sunny, our proud Arabian with a wild streak, and Peanut, who was plump and white with brown markings and scooped nose. Although my uncle argued that Peanut was really a very large pony, she was my favorite mare at the time. Dark brown with black mane and tail, our new colt promised to offer the best of both his parents, gentleness and strength. Daddy let me name him, and I called him Pride.

Dad drove our pickup to the pasture gate, and we climbed out in the crisp air. As I pulled on my gloves, I saw Daddy glance in the direction of the iced-over pond. Peanut stood at the pond's edge, alone. Her ears perked up when she saw us, and she ambled over. Dad spoke to her.

"Hey, girl. Where's your baby?" Peanut answered by simply moving closer to Dad, searching for a treat. She was a big baby herself.

"Get her some oats, I'll find the colt," he said. I ducked into the tack room where the feed was stored, scooped up some of the sweet-smelling feed, and came back out to the barn's main aisle to see Peanut staring into one of our open stalls. I found Dad in the stall, down on his hands and knees, patting Pride, who was lying on his side.

"Come on, boy, stand up," he urged, but Pride didn't respond. Dad put his hands up by the colt's muzzle, over the nostrils. He turned to me with a grim expression. "I think he's frozen." I couldn't believe it.

"Are you sure?" I asked. "Maybe he's asleep." I moved around Pride's head, gently stroked his neck, and ran my fingers through his cool, soft coat. "Wake up, Pride." I wanted to see a quiver, but there was nothing.

"Peanut must have left him alone, and when the temperature dropped down last night, he fell asleep and froze," he said. I looked over at Peanut stuffing herself with oats, oblivious to the plight of her new colt. At that moment, I hated my favorite mare.

"Why did she leave him?" I asked, choking back tears as I continued to stroke Pride's fine coat. Daddy stroked alongside me.

"It's not her fault. She's a new mama, she didn't know any better," he said. I tried not to cry, but a tear escaped, slipped down my cheek, and landed on the motionless colt. Dad must have seen. Suddenly, he put his strong arms under the colt's limp body and scooped him up into his arms.

"Open the tail gate," he ordered. I ran ahead of him to the truck and pulled down the tailgate. Under the weight of the limp colt, Dad lumbered along awkwardly. I scrambled up in the truck bed just before he gently laid the foal next to me.

"Hold onto him," he said. I wrapped my arms tightly around Pride's downy neck, and we pulled off, headed toward our old farmhouse now vacant for the winter. There, I held open the back porch door while my father carried the colt in his arms, up the stairs. What was he doing?

"Open the door," he said. I reached up for the hidden key and unlocked the door. He struggled through the doorway, angling the colt several ways before finally passing into the kitchen. "Open the oven," he instructed. I hesitated. He was scaring me, but I obeyed. Gently, he lifted the colt onto the open oven door, turned the oven on low, and began rubbing his hands back and forth across the colt's body. With heat and love, my dad was trying to coax the colt back to life. I joined him.

"Come on, boy, come on," I said, rubbing the colt's neck and sweet face. Dad and I worked together for some time, but we didn't say much. I felt miserable that I hadn't been there when Peanut had abandoned him. As I worked along with Dad to try and save him, waves of sadness were replaced with a sense of purpose.

The room grew uncomfortably hot, and we stopped working for a moment to slip out of our jackets, then we continued our efforts for another 20 minutes. The colt still didn't move. Dad gave a final pat to Pride's neck and spoke.

"Do you think he's going to come around?" he asked. I ran my hand along Pride's neck one last time, felt the fluffy, cold coat pass under my fingertips. I answered Dad with a somber shake of my head. Despite our efforts, we lost the fight.

We stopped at my uncle's house down the lane to see if he could help Dad bury Pride in the back pasture. Dad explained what had happened, and our efforts to revive the colt in the warm kitchen.

"Now why'd you do a stupid thing like that?" my uncle asked. He had been around farm animals his entire life. "You know you can't bring something frozen back to life. Didn't you learn that in college?" Dad gave me a sidelong glance.

"We needed to try," he said. My uncle shook his head in dismay.

"Craziest thing I ever heard," he said. But I knew my dad wasn't crazy. He had attempted the impossible, for me. I knew, then, how much Dad cared for me.

A few weeks later our prissy Welsh pony, Flicka, was due to foal. Against Mama's strong objections, Dad loaded her up in the trailer and brought her to our city home. Together, we broke up a bale of hay, spread it all around the concrete floor of our garage, which was attached to our house. He unloaded Flicka and took her inside the garage, shut the door against the cold. A few days later, Flicka gave birth to a healthy colt, which I named Banner. For the next few weeks, until the cold passed, our entire house had an overpowering smell, but Dad and I were happy. Mama? She counted the days till spring!

CHRISTMAS REFLECTIONS

Georgia and Tennessee, 1950s-1960s

The most memorable Christmases are not just about the gifts I receive. As I reflect on the many holidays (and they are numerous) I've celebrated with family and friends, only a few memories poke their heads out of the marsh that is my consciousness. Most of them are from childhood.

In the 1950s, my family would head out to the pasture to search for a cedar tree. I remember the crisp and chilly air and the scent of burning wood. Trudging through the pasture, we sized up each cedar we saw, trying to find one that wasn't too tall for our living room yet was big enough to bear the weight of treasured ornaments, colored lights, tinsel, and Chihuahua attacks.

"What about this one?" Daddy would ask. We children discussed the merits of each tree, and eventually we'd mostly agree on one. Daddy and brother Dean chopped down the tree and hoisted it into the truck bed to drive it home. When metal trees came into fashion in 1960, I missed our annual hunt for the perfect tree.

One of my favorite memories is of my grammar school Christmas pageant. Around Halloween, students at Missionary Ridge Elementary began rehearsing carols, with each grade assigned different pieces. On the day of the Christmas pageant, there were two performances. Strains of "It Came Upon a Midnight Clear" and "Hark the Herald, Angels Sing" echoed through the building as each grade sang from several locations—in hallways and standing on stairwells. After each group had finished, students remained in place listening to other grades sing their carols. Finally, during a procession into the school auditorium, all the students carried gifts wrapped in white tissue paper and laid them on the edge of the stage in front of the manger scene featuring sixth graders as Mary and Joseph. I can't remember what was inside the simply wrapped gifts to be given to the needy; I only recall how joyful I felt thinking about the unknown person who would receive the present.

One of my most vivid memories is of the time our church youth fellowship group recreated a nativity scene in front of Brainerd Methodist church, which I attended. Standing in frigid rain and wind along with my friends dressed in costume, we teenagers tried to look solemn as we attempted to convey the feelings of awe at the birth of a savior. We stood still around the manger, cloaked in robes with cargo jackets underneath, acting out the nativity for each passing car of spectators that slowed down to watch. In between viewings, we ran in place and joked about the possibility of icicles forming on our nostrils if it got much colder. We were persistent as the evening grew bitterly cold. When one of the counselors tried to make us go back inside to call it quits, we stubbornly held out, propelled by the fun we were having and a sense of purpose.

Not a December goes by that I don't remember the saddest Christmas I experienced growing up, the time my big brother was hospitalized and couldn't be home to celebrate. Three years older than I was, he was a rambunctious boy and played hard. His taste for adventure sometimes ended with a visit to the doctor's. During the 1960 Christmas school vacation, he and a neighbor boy rode horses and played cowboys and Indians. Wielding a BB gun, the neighbor boy inexplicably aimed at my brother. A BB shattered Dean's eyeglass lenses, propelling glass shards into one of his eyes.

He was rushed to the hospital for surgery and spent the next two weeks of the holiday season lying in bed with bandages on both eyes. The doctor feared that Dean would lose vision in both eyes from the accident, and while everyone else was celebrating the holidays, our parents visited the hospital, while we children mostly waited at home. Dean prayed the entire time that he would be able to see again. That year, I don't remember having many gifts under the tree, or even if there was a tree. That Christmas, I wished for only one gift, for my big brother to keep his vision. When the bandages were finally removed, his vision was blurry. Eventually, the room came into focus, and his sight was restored, although his injured eye would never be 20/20 again. This was the best gift our family could receive. I was thankful.

With the approach of every holiday season, I find myself thinking not about what presents to buy but about memories I can make with family and friends. Will it be caroling and sharing a hot cup of tea or cider after? Will we light candles on Christmas Eve at church and sing "Silent Night" in the soft glow of candlelight? Will we take a neighborhood walk after savoring a Christmas feast and enjoying good company?

The best memories don't seem to cost much. They're free for the making. During every holiday season, I wish each one of you good memories.

SHOW GIRLS

Georgia and Tennessee, 1960s

To me, Peanut was the most beautiful mare in the world. She was fluffy and white with a chocolate brown face and slightly plump from having delivered a foal. With her scooped nose, her face almost looked Arabian, although she was just a mixture of Quarter Horse and Welsh pony.

I was proud of Peanut and wanted to ride her in the pleasure class at the local horse show scheduled for the end of the summer. When Daddy vetoed riding lessons, I tried to explain that English style was different than Western, and I would need to learn English equitation and the ins and outs of what to do in the show ring.

"Don't you want me to show her?" I pleaded. Finally, he agreed that while I could show Peanut, and he would deliver us to the horse show, it was up to me to figure out the rest. I was angry with him but determined to move ahead.

That spring, my best friend Ellen began taking formal riding lessons, so I accompanied her and hung on the fence rail, absorbing all that the teacher told her. I watched how the teacher moved- hands down, erect posture, smooth posting. Ellen and I asked Mama to take us to all the nearby horse shows that spring and summer. There, we observed the horses going through their paces, lining up, and stretching out before the judges.

When summer arrived, and with no practice ring in sight, I asked my uncle to mow out a large circle in the tall field of fescue near our farmhouse. Finally, with my "grass ring" in place, I set out to train Peanut. At first, she was stubborn and fought against my attempts to train her to walk, trot, and canter using leg signals. Before, we'd simply ridden for fun, but now I was insisting she do something that did not come naturally. But after several weeks of practice, she grew accustomed to acting differently in our "ring" and learned that there, I expected her to go through her paces at my command. The thing she resisted most was the line-up and the required stretch-out, a most unnatural position. At first, I had to dismount and nudge her legs forward using my hands while telling her to stretch. When she complied, I'd pet her and speak to her in soothing tones. Eventually, I had to train her to do this when I was in the saddle. It was not an easy task, but she finally stretched when she heard my voice command, combined with a gentle tap of my riding crop on her shoulder to prompt her.

That summer, the imaginary judges who watched Peanut and me in our grass ring demanded perfection from both of us. Through the sweltering summer, we trained day in and out, readying for the horse show, where I expected the judges would appreciate my Peanut by awarding her a blue, red, or white ribbon. They would affirm what I knew already: she was the best horse in the world. Although Peanut, not me, would be judged, I would need to wear a proper English riding outfit to match my well-trained mare. But when I priced the riding habits, I realized a new one was out of my price range. Mama agreed to let me do chores to earn enough to purchase jodhpur boots and jodhpurs. Ellen asked her riding teacher if I could borrow one of her old riding jackets, and she agreed to loan me a faded green jacket, otherwise in good shape.

The day of the show, Dad, Ellen, and I loaded Peanut in the trailer and headed to the exhibition hall in town. We unloaded in a paddock area along with the other horses. Many of them appeared to be purebred Saddlebreds, bigger and sleeker than my Peanut. I told Ellen I was afraid that if these "professional" show horses rode in the pleasure class with us, we didn't stand a chance. Ellen encouraged me and said we would do fine, that those horses were obviously going to show in the other classes, not mine. I appreciated her encouragement, but as I brushed Peanut's white coat and fluffed up her straw-colored tail, I grew increasingly nervous as the time approached for us to enter the ring.

Finally, it was time to queue up. I filed in between two sleek Saddlebreds ridden by equestrians dressed in what appeared to be brand-new riding habits. I glanced down at Peanut's wide girth, at the faded green cuffs of my jacket, and almost turned around. But then I looked up and saw Ellen waving me on. With a burst of fierce pride for my plump, unpolished mare, for her hard work over the summer, I entered the ring determined to win. We'd show them!

As we circled the ring, I focused entirely on the required gaits—walk, trot, and canter—on reversing directions as requested by the judges. I posted smoothly in my saddle, held my head high, as did Peanut. All too quickly, it was time for the final lineup where the judges would study each entrant. Using my toe, I coaxed her into a full stretch and prayed for her to pitch her ears forward like the Saddlebreds on either side of us. The judges walked down the line, scowling at each horse and making notes. Ellen stood by the rail snapping her fingers to get Peanut's attention. Just as the judges walked by, Peanut tipped her ears forward. Finally, the judges had all the riders circle the ring once more at a trot. We lined up again and waited for the results.

First place was called … and second … and third. The top winners were the "professionals" as I had expected. I sat high in the saddle and tried to appear proud and confident, but I felt a deep blush of embarrassment beginning to warm my face. I didn't know how many ribbons would be awarded, but at this point, I simply wanted to get out of that ring. The judge kept handing out the ribbons until there were only three of us left in the line-up. Then I heard my number announced. Applause came from the ringside, and I looked over to see Ellen clapping. I trotted over and graciously accepted the ribbon handed to me: a maroon ribbon with a rosette on top reading: 8th place. We'd won the last possible ribbon, but we'd placed! I trotted Peanut out of the ring and returned to the paddock area and received congratulations from Ellen and Daddy.

While Ellen loaded some film in her camera, I petted Peanut and told her,"Good job." I clipped the maroon ribbon to the side of her bridle. It wasn't the blue, red, or white I'd hoped for. My mare wasn't sleek or polished or purebred, but she'd tried her best. Wearing her maroon ribbon next to her sweet, scooped face, to me, Peanut was still the most beautiful horse in the world.

NEIGHBOR'S GIFT

Tennessee, 1960s

She lived up the street in an aging house, and she was my friend. With her neck permanently bent down at an angle from the ravages of arthritis, Mrs. B. was a kind and welcoming neighbor who invited me into her darkened living room filled with dusty books and ferns. The antimacassars placed on the sturdy chair arms could hide wear and tear, but not the musty smell of passing time. The house was silent except for the sound of a ticking grandfather clock. When Mrs. B. spoke, it was with a voice low and gravelly but always cultured.

Unlike many of our Southern neighbors, she offered nothing to drink or eat. Our conversations were food enough. She would ask me about my day at school, what I liked to study, and what was I reading? I was 10 or 11, and being the youngest of four children, not accustomed to so much attention from someone who had all the time in the world.

If I were lucky, Mrs. B. would take time to recite her favorite poem by the English poet William Blake.

"Tyger, tyger, burning bright.
In the forests of the night;
What immortal hand or eye,
Could frame thy fearful symmetry?"

Enraptured by her clear enunciation, the rise and fall of her voice emphasizing words she thought important, I sat still and listened. I imagined the huge tiger and a dark green jungle filled with ferns, much like those perched on a shelf behind her sofa. I peered through the leafy ferns, hoping to catch a glimpse of the big cat's eyes. She recited the poem in its entirety. Afterward, for a few minutes, we sat in shared silence.

This happened on more than one occasion, and each time Mrs. B. recited her Tyger poem, she seemed to be in another world, in a place and time far away from the confines of her aging house and crooked body. Her hooded blue eyes would fill with light.

Year-round, I stopped at the squeaky, vine-covered gate to enter her yard and climb the stairs to her porch. I'd ring the doorbell, and she would welcome me into her world. One December, when Christmas was approaching, she offered me a seat, and with much mischief in her eyes, she announced she had a gift for me. With faltering steps, she left the living room to retrieve the present from another part of the house. I waited, anticipating what I was about to receive. I let my eyes wander around the room to see the books, the ferns, and the dim light that filtered through the yellowed windows. I knew she didn't have a lot of money, and I wondered if she would give me one of her books, perhaps even the book with the tiger poem. She returned with a rectangular box wrapped in plain white tissue paper, the size of a book. She placed the gift in my hands.

"Would you like to open it now?" she asked.

"Yes," I answered. Although I knew it was a book, I would act surprised when I opened it. This would make her happy. I placed my finger under the seam and ripped up, expecting to see a dusty cover. Instead, I saw yellow and black, some type of label. A box of prunes!

"Oh," was the only word that popped out of my mouth. And a few seconds later, "Thank you."

"You're welcome," she said. "Now, would you like to hear the tiger poem?"

"Yes," I answered. She sat down near me and began with a dramatic flourish.

"Tyger, tyger, burning bright …" On this afternoon, I was not transported to the jungle. All I could think about was the box of prunes sitting on my lap. Why had she given me such an odd gift? I knew enough to act pleased with her gift, even though I was puzzled. I was having a hard time understanding why anyone would wrap up a box of prunes for a child. Didn't she know most children didn't eat prunes? As soon as she finished the tiger poem, I'd thank her and run home to show Mama. Maybe she could make some sense of it.

A half-century has passed since I got that box of prunes, and each passing year brings me nearer to the age she was when I was her neighbor. Unable to drive, and confined to her house, Mrs. B. wanted to share what she had. She took something she liked from her pantry and wrapped it up. She gave me what she had on hand. She was a proper sort of person, well-mannered, and she wanted to participate in a Christmas ritual.

I am ashamed to say I cannot remember if I gave her anything at all. If I did, it was probably something handmade, such as one of my horse drawings. All these years later, I've changed my mind about those prunes. I've come to appreciate their rich, moist flavor, and I'm pleased when someone gives me dried fruit at Christmas. I smile when I think of unwrapping that yellow and black box, yet I realize that gift taught me how to think beyond my expectations, how to receive a present graciously, especially one that seems odd.

I also now realize Mrs. B. was my first literary friend. What has endured is her real gift to me: an appreciation for books and poetry, a love for the cadence of words, and always, a soaring imagination.

DAYS OF ROCK AND ROLL

Tennessee and Georgia, 1960s-1970

During junior high, I was obsessed with the new long-haired band out of England along with my best friend, Ellen, and a group of other young fans. When I heard of a radio contest for tickets to a live concert, I decided I would win. Every night, instead of doing homework, I wrote out 50 entry slips. I did this for a full month and turned them all in. My grades suffered, but of course I won!

One of my classmates also won tickets, and she convinced her dad to drive us to Jacksonville, Florida despite the incoming weather forecast, a hurricane.

I cannot recall the journey, but I can still see our arrival at the hotel where windows were crisscrossed with duct tape. The hurricane had passed, and now Beatlemaniacs stormed the hotel corridors. Their spirit was contagious!

I was in our hotel room when I heard screams coming from below. I raced downstairs and followed the sound to find a group of fans outside surrounding a black limo as it tried to pull out of the hotel garage. I pushed my way through the crowd, saw the fabulous four on the other side, and jumped across the hood to brush my hand against John Lennon's shoulder. I could not believe my good fortune in not only seeing a Beatle up close, but in touching him! I decided not to wash my hand for days.

From the Beatles onward, I was hooked on popular music and along with my big brother, listened to it all day long except when I was in school. In late June 1970, my friends and I heard of a Woodstock-type music festival down in Georgia, so on the spur of the moment we decided to go, although Mama didn't approve. I was 19, I told Mama, and free to do whatever I wanted. Grabbing a pair of extra jeans and some Goo Goo Clusters, I hopped into one of the boys' vans and set out for the Macon area. About halfway there, the traffic thickened as thousands of hippies and music lovers descended on the tiny town of Byron, Georgia, the festival site.

We were lucky to find a spot in the woods among many other vans and tents. Passing through a haze of pot smoke and numerous topless men and some women, we followed the sounds of guitar and voices to find the stage. There, for the next three days, we listened to the Allman Brothers, Jethro Tull, B.B. King, Ravi Shankar, Richie Havens, Procol Harum, and Jimi Hendrix. We partied with other young people, linked together by our love of music and the freedom to do as we pleased, which in some cases meant getting high. Pot and alcohol were easily available, and drug dealers sold LSD, mescaline, and magic mushrooms to anyone with the money, and sometimes gave it away to cute girls. As we walked through the woods, I was shocked to see stoned, naked men and women, their limbs entwined like pretzels, "hiding" behind the pine trees. Those trees did not hide a thing. I made a mental note to stick to beer and only from unopened cans or bottles. I'd stay away from Kool-Aid, freely offered, which was laced with LSD.

Two nights sleeping in the cramped van, overexposure in 100-degree heat, and a lack of sleep began to take its toll. My skin was bright red and blistering, and I stunk from not bathing. We heard an epidemic of hepatitis had broken out, so we stayed away from the swimming pool and creek. There was no drinking water, and all we had to drink was Coke or beer. People were overdosing left and right. Governor

Maddox flew over the festival site and declared it a disaster. Our adventure was becoming scarier by the hour. From a pay phone, I called Mama collect. She advised me to leave the festival, get a motel room with my girlfriends, clean up, and get some rest.

After showers and a night in real beds, we returned to the festival. We staked out a spot in front of the stage amidst the crowd and listened to music all day and into the night. Just before midnight, I drifted off, only to wake up to the energetic chords of an electric guitar. I sat up to see Jimi Hendrix playing "The Star-Spangled Banner." The fireworks exploded above in the night sky. As I heard Hendrix play, felt the energy of the crowd, and saw the fireworks, I knew this was a magical night, a time that I felt free, a moment I would never forget.

RUNNING FOR LOVE

California, 1970s

Seeking the California dream in the 1970s, I migrated west, ultimately landing at the University of California, Berkeley, a giant school that offered the journalism major that I so desperately wanted. While there, I met a young man named Steve, who enjoyed an adventure as much as I.

Standing in a large crowd gathered around the campanile one night, Steve and I waited for the rumored streakers to appear. He hoisted me up on his shoulders just in time to witness a single, naked man flash past like he was running the 50-yard dash. The crowd roared in approval.

"Tell me what you see," Steve said.

"Not much. He's running too fast," I answered. A few days later, inspired not by the streaker's nudity but by his speed, Steve and I decided to take up running. We would start running up the Strawberry Canyon fire trail into the Berkeley hills that overlooked the Bay Area.

When I first met him, I had been impressed by Steve's athletic abilities. He played handball, fenced, and could jog backwards. Me? I was lucky to huff and puff along to Evans Hall on my old English bike. I wasn't out of shape, but I wasn't exactly in shape, either.

The first day of our routine we set off on the densely wooded trail at a brisk walk. After about five minutes, Steve, who knew the rules on all things athletic, told me that next we should jog, eventually working our way up to a run.

"But if you get tired before the top, you can walk for a few minutes, then jog again," he said.

"And the same for you, if you get tired," I answered. He laughed.

"I'll wait for you at the top," he said, and took off at a steady pace. I watched him move ahead out of sight, then looked down at my new sneakers pounding steadily along the dirt path and vowed to show him I was just as strong as he. I had always prided myself on being able to run with the boys, and Steve was no exception. Since I had met him, we had gone spelunking in a dark and deep cave and whitewater rafting. Although running together would be a way to get fit, what I really wanted was to show Steve that I could keep up with him.

After jogging uphill for a mile, I began to run out of breath and decided to walk. It felt good to slow down and get my breath again. I thought about the view at the top—a sweeping panorama of the shimmery, silver bay and San Francisco beyond. No doubt Steve was already at the top, enjoying the view, and more annoyingly, resting while I hadn't even made it up halfway. I moved into a steady jog again and continued upward, trying to distract myself with the sight of tall oak trees along the way and the fresh smells of the forest. But once again, each breath seemed to burn as I inhaled, so remembering what Steve had said, I slowed down to a walk.

Finally, seeing the trail top near, and thinking he might see me slacking off, I broke into a full run, an easy feat at this point since I was no longer winded from my walk-jog-walk routine. I arrived at the top and ran right past him, further into the woods, along the steep trail.

"Whew!" I said as I passed him. "I finally made it."

"Yes, and you didn't even break much of a sweat," he replied.

"Isn't that great?" I said, taking his hand. "Let's go look at the view of the bay."

We continued our running kick all that fall, and into the spring, or rather he continued running, and I continued my version of running—mostly a jog-walk-jog, always with an impressive burst of running at the end. Every time, he beat me to the top and even continued to run deep into the woods beyond our stopping point. As I reached the top of the trail, he soon appeared to take in the view with me. Often, he would remark on how well I was doing.

"Watts, you're not even perspiring," he'd say as he wiped his wet brow with a handkerchief.

"I guess I'm just in better shape than you," I'd tease.

"Maybe," he said. "But why do I always beat you to the top?" I pointed to his long tan limbs.

"Longer legs?" I replied. He laughed.

After graduation, right before we moved away, we took our final run up Strawberry Canyon. When I reached the top, I headed toward our usual place to take in the view of the bay, but Steve took my hand and led me to a clearing behind some trees. He pointed toward the trail where we'd run for the past nine months.

"Nice view of the trail," I said. "You can see all the runners coming up."

"And walkers," he said, a sly grin on his face.

PICTURE HAT

California, 1970s

After dating for three years, Steve and I decided to marry. We planned a small California church wedding with a Southern flair and a fancy dress.

Mama and I were at the final fitting for my wedding gown in Hollywood. The seamstress, Madame, a bouncy French woman, held up a skein of pink ribbon next to my face.

"Pink is much better for your skin tone, don't you think, Mademoiselle?" asked Madame in her heavily accented English.

"Yes," I answered. But I really wasn't thinking about the trim for my wedding gown. Instead, I kept wondering who would "give me away" during the wedding ceremony. Originally, I had asked my father, and he had agreed but later changed his mind. Although my parents had been divorced for several years, emotions still ran high. Mama's thick Southern drawl interrupted my thoughts.

"Can we see the hat?" Mama asked. Reared as a Southern belle, Mama had thrown herself full throttle into my wedding plans. She envisioned a *Gone with the Wind-style* ensemble. Madame brought over a round hatbox and placed it on Mama's lap with a dramatic flourish.

"Voila," she said, gesturing for Mama to open the lid. Mama gently removed the lid and pulled out the widest-brimmed hat I'd ever seen. I reached in and pulled out the hat, placed it on my head, and turned so Mama could see. She clapped her hands together and sighed.

"Perfect," she said. But I wasn't so sure. With its layers of lace and ribbon, the hat seemed a bit frilly. And that brim? Broad enough to use as an umbrella. Excited about my oversized chapeau, Mama chatted with the seamstress as she pinned on pink ribbon. Mama hadn't had a fancy wedding herself, and she seemed so excited about my Southern belle ensemble. I glanced into the mirror at the picture hat and the wide hem of my gown. So old-fashioned, but not that bad. Besides, it was too late to order anything else. I turned my thoughts to my other dilemma--would I end up giving myself away?

A week before the wedding, Mama and I had dinner with our future in-laws. Learning of my dilemma, my father-in-law-to-be graciously offered to be my escort.

"I'd be proud to walk you down the aisle," he stated in his husky voice, gazing at me with his deep brown eyes. I appreciated his offer, and his sincerity made me want to cry, but I couldn't let him. How could he "give the bride away" when he wasn't my family, not yet? We discussed an uncle, but no one felt right for the task. No solution seemed in sight until my fiancé, Steve, spoke.

"Why does it have to be a man?" he asked. I thought about it. It was the late 1970s, but most of the weddings I'd ever attended had been steeped in tradition. I'd never seen anyone except a man perform the hand-off. My future father-in-law shook his head in dismay, clearly disapproving of his son's idea. Steve reached out and touched Mama's shoulder.

"I think it should be you," said Steve. Mama beamed, but I didn't know what to say.

"I'd love to," Mama said, "if the bride wants me to." Everyone turned to look at me, and I looked back at Mama. A petite 5′2″, she seemed to have grown an inch taller at the mere suggestion.

"Why not?" I said. Mama grinned. I smiled too but thought it wasn't a good idea. I'd never seen a mother give away the bride!

A week later at the rehearsal, Mama went through the paces flawlessly. Still, I worried about our wedding day. What would our guests think?

The wedding day arrived. A bit nervous, I proceeded down the aisle of the church. Wrapped in a cloud of rainbow pastel voile, Mama calmly waited for me in the front. Seeing her, I moved ahead confidently. She stepped out of the pew and into the aisle to offer me her arm. Together, we walked over to my groom. Then she did something she hadn't rehearsed. She took both his hands in hers, looked him hard in the eyes as if to say, "You had better take good care of my daughter."

After the wedding, when we were taking pictures, Mama leaned in under the wide brim to kiss me. When she pulled away, the hat tipped and almost fell off, but Mama helped me put it back on. We both laughed at the "tipsy hat."

In the reception line, everyone congratulated Mama on doing a good job giving me away. My picture hat was a big hit.

Today, when I look at the frilly hat, I can see Mama's big smile, hear her laughter. With its lace and ribbon, the picture hat is delicate and traditional, so unlike Mama, a woman ahead of her time, brave enough to carry off a "man's job" with dignity and grace.

GOLD DUST TWINS

Tennessee, 2002

When my niece was killed in a tragic accident, I was devastated. She was my firstborn niece, and I had known her since she came into this world. Not only was she smart and lovely, but she was also a wife and mother with young children. A tragedy for her family and anyone who knew her.

I called Ellen, my best friend, and flew to Memphis for the funeral. Ellen jumped into her car and drove for eight hours to meet me. She arrived at the hotel with a big hug and a cake. Not just any old cake, but the date nut cake she's been baking since we were children.

Ellen and I could not have come from more different backgrounds. Ellen's home was immaculate and run by her well-organized mother and a full-time housekeeper. All five girls were expected to conform to the role of proper young Southern ladies, excelling in school, taking piano lessons, and most of all helping those in need. All of them were taught to bake at an early age, and I was amazed when I watched Ellen bake a date nut cake from scratch by reading her Granny's recipe.

My home, on the other hand, was often messy and filled with kids and dogs and sometimes a pony. To Mama, cooking was a terrible chore to be endured. She was lucky to just get three meals a day on the table. There was no time or energy for frills like baking. Besides, Mama did not teach us traditional feminine tasks like cooking. Instead, she encouraged us to paint, dance freestyle, make up plays, and explore the woods on horseback. She made sure we had plenty of free time, which she felt encouraged creativity. I often entertained myself while my older sisters and brother played with their friends. Shy and quiet, I spent most of my time with my dogs or pony, but what I really wanted was a sister my own age.

In third grade, I found one. Like me, Ellen had long blonde hair she wore in a ponytail. We both loved horses and books, and she was also the fourth child, but in her case, one of five sisters. Soon, we were inseparable, and we declared ourselves best friends. With a twinkle in her eye, Mrs. Pennington, our third-grade teacher, dubbed us "The Gold Dust Twins."

Ellen enjoyed coming to my house, where she enjoyed my mother's "free spirit" style. I, on the other hand, enjoyed going to Ellen's because everything seemed so orderly and structured. I felt safe knowing what was expected of me.

As the years passed, despite our different backgrounds, our friendship grew, although our paths diverged. She was sent to a private girls' school, and I went to public. We didn't see each other as often, but we grew closer with phone calls and letters where we shared the secrets and travails of our unfolding lives.

When I was 17, my parents separated. With my older siblings off at college, it was just Mama and me alone in our almost empty house. Since Mama had not yet found a full-time job, money was tight and groceries a luxury. One day, Ellen showed up with several bags of groceries, the ingredients for her Granny's date nut cake, she said. But there was also fresh fruit, cheese, and meat. Mama was thrilled and thanked her as she put away the groceries. Ellen and I chopped dates and nuts and talked as she whipped up the cake. She tried to show me how to read the recipe, to carefully time the glaze frosting until it reached the "soft ball" stage, whatever that meant. Ellen and I were so busy laughing and carrying on that I never really took time to understand the chemistry of baking.

For the next few months, Ellen kept showing up with bags of groceries, just enough to keep Mama and I going until she got a full-time teaching position. We enjoyed her visits as much as the food, and the cakes she baked.

We were still best friends when I moved to California for college. Ellen and I each made other friends, found husbands, and had children. Over the years we kept up our friendship by talking on the phone and writing letters and sometimes flying out to visit one another. We exchanged presents, and every few years, I ripped open her birthday package to find a tasty date nut cake nestled into a tin, a tasty reminder of our enduring friendship.

So, when my niece died, and Ellen showed up with the cake, I felt comforted and very much loved. We talked and cried while we ate the date nut cake and reminisced.

Through the years, joys and sorrows, we "Gold Dust Twins" have remained close, although I am ashamed to say I never did learn to bake a cake from scratch. Time and distance have not lessened the friendship between two little girls who found gold in each other and discovered the alchemy of friendship through a cake lovingly shared.

A MARE CALLED SNIP

Georgia, 1861-1865

I remember spending my summers down in Woodstation, Georgia, riding my horses in a big field in front of my grandmother's house. She would sit on her front porch in her rocking chair and watch me canter through the tall fescue. I rode constantly, in the heat of muggy days and into the evening to the cicadas' serenade. When it became too dark to see, I'd climb off my horse, go sit with Grandma, and listen to her stories of the past.

More than once, Grandma told me that loving horses ran in our family. Some of the men in our family had ridden in the cavalry. But the story I liked best was the one about *her* grandmother who had lived through the Civil War.

The days and nights must have been long for Matilda Arnold Seabolt while her husband McKinney fought along with the Georgia 23rd Infantry Regiment up north. A young mother in her 20s, Matilda lived with her parents in Naomi, Georgia, a small community tucked in the valley next to the long and low-slung Taylor's Ridge. She cared for her small daughter, Addie, and doted on her favorite horse, a fine gray mare she called Snip.

Matilda had heard stories about a band of irregulars called the Gatewood Scouts who terrorized the area and took whatever they could—hogs, chickens, eggs, flour, and horses. In rural areas of the South, mules and horses were especially valuable since they were the only way to get around. Horses and mules also helped fight the Civil War, and many died in battle or from disease.

Hearing the Gatewood Scouts were in the area, and fearing for her mare's safety, Matilda hid Snip in the deep woods near Taylor's Ridge.

Soon, the band of scouts arrived at Matilda's family farm and stole bushels of potatoes and fruit, syrup, tobacco, and hogs. When one of them took little Addie's red bucket, she cried. Seeing her tears, the scout relented and gave it back. By the time they were ready to depart, the scouts had rounded up several horses they wanted, but before they left, they somehow found out about the mare in hiding. They demanded the horse be brought to them at once. When Matilda refused, they threatened to burn down her family's house. Fearing the loss of her home, she asked her father, Billy Arnold, to retrieve Snip from the woods. When he returned, the scouts announced that they were taking the horse and heading south to Calhoun, about 15 miles away.

To everyone's surprise, Matilda jumped up on Snip's wide back and told the soldiers she would ride the horse herself. The scouts asked her to dismount, but she refused, saying that wherever her horse went, so did she. She told them she intended to stay with the horse to ensure she was cared for properly. Off they rode, a ragtag group: the band of men and one very determined Southern woman aboard her mare. They headed up Taylor's Ridge into the twilight.

Through the long night they rode, the men pleading with her to get off her horse. She wouldn't budge. The men told her they didn't want to hurt her but that she had to get off and return home. She clung onto Snip's long mane and kept up with the scouts' pace.

By the time dawn approached, the scouts must have realized they had never seen such a stubborn woman. Fearing that daylight would reveal them to the locals, the scouts finally gave up and rode away, leaving behind Matilda, still aboard her mare. Her determination had paid off. She wheeled her horse around and headed home.

Later, she would mourn for her husband who was killed at the Battle of Antietam. And still later, she was saddened when the South lost the war. But through it all, her courage and resolve kept her beloved Snip close and safe.

I have never seen a picture of Snip, but I have seen one of my great-great-grandmother. Her pretty face is full of energy and confidence. I would have liked to have known her, so I could have thanked her for the legacy she left: tenacity and a spunky spirit.

MORE CIVIL WAR ANCESTORS

Georgia, 1861-1865

In North Georgia, history seems to ooze out of the very soil. Monuments dot the landscape, reminders of the troops who fought the Civil War battles. The ground offers up the occasional Minié ball or button. In our families, tombstones and reunions keep history alive, offering clues to ancestral puzzles that beg to be solved. What part did family members play in the Civil War?

My great-grandfather John Berry Watts came to Catoosa County, Georgia to fight in the Battle of Chickamauga. He had joined in Union County, Georgia in April 1862 and was a sergeant in Company B, 6th Georgia Cavalry. The following month, his father, William E. Watts, and his brother, James L. Watts, joined the same company.

During the war, great-grandfather Watts served as a reconnaissance officer. One family story tells of the time he was scouting on horseback up in the Fort Oglethorpe area. Union troops spotted him and began firing. He galloped away as fast as he could, lying down with his head against the horse's neck to avoid being hit. Another story describes the time when great-grandfather was taking a position in a cabin up at the Chickamauga Battlefield. He and his buddy were firing their weapons through the cracks. A Yankee bullet came through the walls, bounced off a log and hit his friend. Thinking he had been mortally wounded, the buddy said, "I'm going to die. Tell my family I love them." My great-grandfather kept shooting but eventually found a chance to turn around and check on his friend. He pulled up the fellow's shirt and saw that the bullet had hit the belt buckle. Great-grandfather told him, "You're not wounded. Get up and fight." Or so the story goes …

In January of 1865, John Berry Watts took a few days off from his military duties to marry Julia Ann (Lilla) Pitner. Four months later in May, after Confederate General Joe Johnston surrendered to General Sherman, Watts was dismissed from service at Greensboro, North Carolina. After the war, he returned to the area and settled in Walker County with his family, and later moved to Woodstation. Ten years after he left the service, he and Lilla had their fifth child, my grandfather, James Melvin Watts.

What I best remember about great-grandfather was a story my father told me about a corn cob pipe that great-grandfather and other vets received when they gathered sometime after the war. I also know he enjoyed sporting a long beard after the war because I've seen photos of him.

While great-grandfather Watts was busy fighting alongside the Rebels, another grandfather was trying hard to stay out of the fray. My Grandma Watts' grandfather, my great-great-grandfather Harvey M. Williams, was sympathetic to the Union. He farmed on his 50 acres in Woodstation and made wagons, some of which ended up in the hands of the Yankees. Unlike his five brothers who served in the Confederate army, he avoided conscription by hiding out when the boys in gray came near. Often, he stayed out in the woods, waiting for them to pass. Other times he stayed at friends' or neighbors' homes. After the Battle of Chickamauga, he took his wagons up to the battlefield to carry away the wounded.

After the war, Grandfather Williams filed a claim to recover for sheep and two mules taken by Union troops. Part of the claim process required him to prove that he was a good Union man. Four witnesses testified that he was, in fact, loyal to the Union, and one stated that Williams had to "lie out to keep them (the Confederates) from hanging him."

One witness, neighbor Pressley Yates, who lived a mile and a half from great-great-grandfather, said, "He preferred the Union to any government. He was never accused of being a Rebel, and we all thought him strictly loyal to the old government." The Southern Claims Commission found Williams to be loyal and awarded him $260 for the mules but didn't give him anything for the sheep.

Another great-great-grandfather, McKinney Seabolt, left the Walker County area to fight at Antietam, also known as Sharpsburg. He was most likely killed in the cornfield battle. He left behind a baby girl, Addie Estella Seabolt, my great-grandmother, who grew up within view of Taylor's Ridge.

Down in the Smyrna area, another great-great-grandfather, Alvin Green Dempsey, really didn't want to join the Confederate army but did. His father, Lazarus Dempsey (my great-great-great-grandfather), was known to be a Union man, and the younger Dempsey joined up to avoid being arrested for his father's Union sentiments. He served as a chaplain in Company A of the 18th Georgia Infantry.

In the summer of 1864, when Sherman's troops arrived in Cobb County near Lazurus Dempsey's place, he had to evacuate. Dempsey, 73, left his home and 40-acre farm and went to DeKalb County. Upon his return home, Lazarus Dempsey found his house gone—disassembled piece by piece—for the Union army's use. His 30 acres of woods had been chopped down. His story came alive for me when I read his deposition in his $875 claim for lost property during the war.

"At the beginning of the rebellion, all my sympathies were with the Union cause. I thought the war would ruin the country. I thought of what General Washington said about breaking the Union. I felt that when we divided, the country was ruined." He continued, "After the ordinance of secession was passed, I still adhered to the Union cause. I never seceded myself. I was a Union man then, and I am a Union man now."

In his testimony, Lazarus Dempsey described the arrival of General Sherman's army that camped within half a mile of his house, north of Decatur, for 48 days and nights. "They were all over the country around there like black birds." As soon as they arrived, they took 100-200 pounds of "good, sound dry bacon." They also stole a mule his grandson was riding on the road in DeKalb County. He estimated the value of the mule at $200. "I am a judge of good mules, and this was a number one mule." He summed it up this way, "This is all I know about the mule. The mule was taken after the bacon was taken, the year of the surrender, I think." Despite Lazarus Dempsey's detailed account and flair for language, and testimony by witnesses on his behalf, the claim was disallowed.

Growing up in the South, I had always assumed that since my family lived here, they were all for the Confederate cause. Thanks to historical documents, I now know otherwise.

Reading the details of my ancestors' struggles brought the Civil War to life for me. I can see one grandfather lying out in the woods to avoid being hanged by the Rebel troops, while another is fighting for the Confederacy and his life up at Chickamauga. I can see old Lazarus pining away for that good, sound dry bacon and his number one mule.

Whatever side they were on 160 years ago doesn't seem to matter now. Differences have been laid to rest, as have the men themselves. And in the case of my Catoosa

County kin, great-grandfather John Berry Watts, Rebel sergeant, and great-great-grandfather Harvey M. Williams, a Unionist, they have ended up in the same Woodstation cemetery, buried mere yards from one another, resting together, at peace at last.

CARMICHAEL HOUSE—MAMA'S FAMILY

Georgia, 1897-Present

Standing in front of the stairs of this more than a century-old mansion, I catch glimpses of reunions past. Youngsters and oldsters smile at the camera, capturing the extended Carmichael family at a happy moment in time. Front and center is my Great Uncle J.R. Carmichael, the son of the man who built this home in 1897 to accommodate his growing family. Atlanta architects Bruce and Morgan designed and built the house from 1897-1898 at a cost of $16,000. Sitting on two and a half acres, the house has 12 rooms, five porches, 10 fireplaces, five chimneys, 47 doors and 77 windows. Mr. and Mrs. J.R. Carmichael, Sr. lived there with their 11 children. The oldest was my grandmother and the sister to one of the youngest children, J.R., my great-uncle.

To anyone who has ever visited the Carmichael house, it's more than just a house on the historic register. Those visitors lucky enough to have stopped by in the 1970s and 1980s enjoyed the personal tours led by J.R. and his wife, Norma Keyes Carmichael. The gracious couple would welcome visitors through the nine-feet high double doors and give a room-by-room tour explaining the design details of fireplaces, or the history of each piece that furnished the rooms, such as the old Victrola. Uncle J.R. loved demonstrating the bell system that ran from the kitchen to other rooms and was used to summon servants to bring snacks upstairs. Aunt Norma enjoyed showing off the *Gone with the Wind* room filled with memorabilia from the movie in which Norma's sister, actress Evelyn Keyes, played the role of Sue Ellen. My mother's favorite spot in the house was the kitchen pantry, where as a child she spent hours watching the cook roll out biscuits on the top of the old butcher block table. As for me, I loved the glassed-in back porch where I cradled my infant son in my arms while Uncle J.R. and Norma served my family iced tea and chilled peaches. When asked how they kept such a big house clean, they spoke of *their* servants.

"Our servants spend every day cleaning a different room," J.R. answered. "Those two are hard workers," he'd add with a wink. I never saw these mysterious servants and finally realized that the elderly couple standing before me were the "servants."

The house has been in my life since I was a child of two, and Mama took me to visit her grandmother, Rosa Anne Kinard Carmichael. Although she was 86, Grandma Carmichael had made me a blue taffeta dress and a fried chicken dinner, so I could remember her. Her plan worked. I do not remember the fried chicken, but I never forgot the silky powder blue dress or the loving hands that created it.

The home is wrapped in porches where our family spent many hours. While aunts and uncles sat in rockers or chairs and talked, cousins rocked in swings and laughed. No visit to the house was complete until my mother insisted on showing me the red clay tennis court where she played growing up. To Mama, tennis was not tennis unless it was played on clay courts.

But for visiting children, the real draw was not the house itself but its vast underbelly. At the front entrance of the house, on either side of the stairs, latticework hides the under porch, a not-too-tall area where Uncle J.R. once rode in goat carts out of sight to casual passersby. In later years, my son Jack and his cousins played hide and seek there in the cool shade out of the summer heat.

The Carmichaels were a prosperous family then with Grandfather owning the bank, a guano factory, and a buggy factory

The large family that enjoyed success was not always happy. Two of the children died before growing up, bringing much sorrow to their parents. Great-Grandfather Carmichael woke up one final morning, walked into a mill pond, and drowned himself, leaving behind an explanatory note that was anything but.

Can a family ever really understand why one of its members takes his own life? I am still trying to figure it out.

Many years of widowhood passed for Grandmother Carmichael, and during the Depression, she turned some of the rooms into apartments to rent out. She passed away in 1953, but not until she had sewn a blue taffeta dress for one of her great-granddaughters. After he retired in 1966, my Great Uncle J.R. undertook the restoration of the house, along with his wife Norma Keyes Carmichael. They moved into the house in 1973. J.R.'s childhood home became his passion in his later life. He and Norma had no children to nurture but instead lavished the Carmichael House with loving care and attention and helped it grow into its place in history.

After Norma's death, and with his own health failing, Uncle J.R. moved out of the house and into a care facility. A few years later, he passed away. The house was sold and transformed into a bed and breakfast. Several years later, it was sold again to new owners who reared their children and occasionally opened the house for special functions.

Today when I stand at the front stairs of the Carmichael house, in a strange confluence of time and memories, I can see Uncle J.R. racing the goat carts underneath the porch, my grandmother descending the elegant staircase to take her vows, and my own son and his cousin playing hide and go seek. I can hear the laughter of generations of children, the ringing of bells that summoned snacks, and scratchy-sounding music playing on the old Victrola in the parlor.

A few years ago, the house that holds more than 128 years of family memories sold once again to a young couple who created a wedding venue and offered teas at Christmas and Mother's Day. Just as the Carmichael family has changed over the years, so the life of the house may change again at some point. I cannot predict the future, but it's a sure bet that no one will be racing goats under the porch any time soon. I know Uncle J.R. would be glad his claim to that fun kind of mischief remains unchallenged.

THE CHANGING PLACE I LEFT BEHIND

Tennessee, Early 2000s

Three and a half decades after I moved to California, I found myself drawn back to Chattanooga, to its vibrant downtown area, to the new center of the city I left behind. I was lured in by the wide river that is like the city itself, always moving, changing, although we cannot see it unless we are up close and take time to look.

But this is not what I thought in 1971 when I was a sophomore at the new University of Tennessee in Chattanooga (UTC). Anti-war protests were erupting all over the country, and change was in the air. Like many college students at that time, I was restless to leave the South, to be anywhere else but my hometown. I longed to move to a more sophisticated and "hipper" place. I moved to California after a visit to my big sister's sunny, ocean-view home during winter break.

In the early 2000s, I found myself back in splashing distance of the water as the "duck" vehicle I rode in plunged down a steep incline into the Tennessee River. As we glided by the art gallery and stately manses, I thought about the changes that had taken place since I left.

Growing up in the fifties and sixties, my world was centered in Brainerd and the area around the Missionary Ridge Tunnel where my dad had his drugstore, Tunnel Drug Store. The stores and shops along Brainerd Road were older and established, but still quite popular. But by the end of the 1960s, the focus shifted to the newly built Eastgate Mall. With its anchor stores of Loveman's and Penney's, Eastgate began to lure shoppers away from the Brainerd Road area, and after the MYF fellowship Sunday night, teenagers migrated near the mall area to hang out at Bob's Big Boy.

When I started high school in the fall of 1966, I traveled across the river by bus to the new City High and discovered a part of Chattanooga I had not known before. I had to transfer buses downtown, and I did so as quickly as possible. Downtown was an area best avoided, unless you happened to attend UTC, or unless you were going over to the rambling, elegant, and old city library on McCallie

Avenue. Going down by the river or to the downtown area was best done in daylight, or in the company of friends.

In the 1980s, I returned to Chattanooga with two small sons who were in their "trains, boats, and planes" phase. We visited the Choo-Choo area where I had greeted my big sister arriving home from college in the 1960s. My sons were disappointed that there were no actual moving trains, but were delighted to spend the night in the hotel train cars nearby. I further appeased them by taking them to ride the steam train over in another part of town, and I was happy someone had thought to put it back in service.

In the early 1990s, I arrived back to enthusiastic chatter about a new, huge mall. I was surprised to find one of my favorite restaurants, The Olive Garden, and stores I knew from out West now within driving distance of my old home place. My visits during the 1990s seemed to center around meeting friends and family somewhere at Hamilton Place Mall or trying to find old landmarks. On one visit, my best friend Ellen showed me Missionary Ridge Elementary School, our alma mater, which she explained would soon be condominiums. On another visit, I was shocked to see it had burned down. As I looked at the ruins, the sounds of Christmas pageants past echoed in my ears. In another visit in the late 1990s, she drove me to visit her father in his new home at Heritage Landing. I did not realize homes could be so close to the water, that flooding fears of the past no longer seemed to be an issue. We visited the Coolidge Park area where the coffee shops and hubbub of activity reminded me of Sausalito, California. It was in the 1990s that I began to feel the excitement of a tourist discovering a new place, the bewilderment of a native finding old that is new.

Around the turn of the century, I found myself drawn back to my hometown not for what I remembered of its past but for its culture. On a visit to the Bluff View Arts District, I sat sipping tea at the Renaissance Commons late one night and glanced around at the diverse crowd that reminded me of L.A. or San Francisco. I sat up and took notice of my native city and what it was becoming. I made a mental note for future visits: I would approach the city like a tourist, looking for the new and different, and not just the familiar.

In 2003, I returned for the Southern Literature Conference where I heard one of my favorite authors, Jill McCorkle, speak. There, I met writers and readers whose knowledge of literature was refreshing to ears accustomed to the film-obsessed culture that is L.A. As part of the same conference, I attended a performance of a Tennessee Williams play at a theatre by the river. The performance was as good, if not better, than any I'd seen out West. At UTC, I attended a poetry reading at a large gymnasium I had remembered from my college days there in early 1970. Then, when the building and I were both younger I had danced between its new walls to Iron Butterfly's "In-a-gadda-da-vida" as part of a modern dance performance. I visited the Bluff View Arts District and walked past the Hunter Art Gallery and a nearby secret spot where friends and I had gathered in our youth to watch boats float by on the river.

At my 35th high school reunion held at the Bluff View Commons, I got a closer view of the new heart of the city. The nighttime view of the river rivaled any I've seen on my travels. Staying at The Chattanoogan, we were pampered with amenities I did not know I could find in my hometown. Floating in a rooftop pool, I found myself bragging to my son about *my* town. While I was out experiencing the world, Chattanooga had grown up behind my back, like a sibling left behind.

Later, we found ourselves shopping for Provence placemats, running to buy coffee, and stopping at the health food store for almonds. We enjoyed returning to my new favorite spots, all near the river area or in the Bluff View Arts

District. We lingered in the sculpture garden and meandered along the river walk, thick with foliage and views of the river at ground level, up close.

On another visit, we checked out of a hotel early just as a hurricane was headed toward Florida. As we walked across the driveway, a Mercedes with Florida plates pulled up. An older couple climbed out, telling the bellman they came to Chattanooga to escape the storm. They had decided they might as well stay in Chattanooga. They said it is a refuge, a place they know well, and it has plenty of things to do. I couldn't have phrased it better myself.

As we headed out of Chattanooga, I found myself sad to leave. I hadn't yet seen the African-American Museum or the IMAX Theater. I realized that my hometown had acquired the sophisticated things I like in L.A.—the arts, good restaurants, and a variety of shops—without so much congestion and with a lot more charm.

Chattanooga, like the river itself, is ever changing, although I did not always stop to notice. And oddly enough, I realized that while I was away for so long, my hometown had become, in many ways, the place I left to find.

GREAT EXPECTATIONS

"Any place that we love becomes our world." —Oscar Wilde

Georgia, 2007

After a 35-year romance, I was starting to fall out of love with California where I'd moved for college. Take two, six plus earthquakes, annual wildfires, mudslides, a dab of smog, and a large cup of homesickness, and I had the recipe for wanting to leave Southern California. I was sure the pace would be slower down in Catoosa County, Georgia, and I could pick right back up where I left off 35 years ago, riding horses, strolling in the countryside, sitting on the porch sipping iced tea and watching June bugs by day, fireflies by night. In between visits with my North Georgia cousins, aunts and uncles, I'd write. My move back to the country would bring me precious hours I never seemed to find in L.A. Everyone knows the South moves at a slower pace, right?

And best of all I'd breathe in the fresh air I'd remembered from my days in the country back in the day. I got the fresh air.

Living down here in the country takes a lot of effort. First of all, the distance between where I live, Woodstation, and everything else—post office, banks, grocery store and restaurants—all in Ringgold, was still eight miles. So, if you forget something on your list, you have to turn around and drive back or do without.

But the road to town never seemed that long when I was younger. I'd simply sit in the back seat and stare out at the passing farms and Taylor's Ridge, all with Daddy or Mama at the wheel. But now it was me and plenty of traffic going up and down to Ringgold. Where had all the cars come from? I know that Catoosa County is fast growing, but why did everyone else seem to need to drive to Ringgold, or back, at precisely the same time I did? And why-oh-why did that teenager in the pickup truck that zoomed ahead of me dangle his arm out the window and shoot me a bird for no apparent reason? I was angry for about 10 seconds until I realized it was a strong reminder that I needed to trade in my California plates for those of my new state: Georgia.

I pulled into the grocery store parking space to find the perfect parking space for me. "Expectant mothers." After all, I am a mother, and I expect wonderful things to happen in my new life. Oh, there's a stork on the sign. Oh, that kind of expectant … I left that space for those ladies expecting something a little more tangible.

I left that space and easily found another, something that would not have happened in L.A. In the parking lot of my former Palisades grocery store, I witnessed arguments and sometimes fender benders between shoppers vying for spaces, all caught on the store's security cameras, along with movie stars buying groceries. My favorite experience was bumping carts with Billy Crystal on Christmas Eve one year as I rolled past the coffee section. But I digress …

Spotting movie stars was the last thing on my mind as I drove down the 151 to my new home tucked in a subdivision in the ridges. My body had arrived in Georgia, but my brain was spinning around inside my head. Moving this far, and to such a very different place, had left me with an odd sensation, as if I'd arrived, but my brain had fallen out somewhere along the way, say Amarillo, Texas. It was like having a bad case of jet lag, or in this case, moving lag.

Things were so familiar yet not so familiar, or déjà vu and new. Our home, for example, was located where I rode horses in the 1960s. The forest where Mama had warned me to watch out for rattlesnakes now had asphalt roads snaking through, populated with Beamers, SUVs, and XL-cab trucks. In days gone by, I'd taken nature hikes in the nearby woods searching for squirrels or deer or heron. Now, in these same woods, the only wildlife I encountered was ATVs that nearly ran me over as I walked on the trails. The riders confronted me and asked what *I* was doing there and informed me I was trespassing. I must admit I was surprised since my family has owned these woods since the 1960s, and the land is posted. Things change, I reminded myself, but the next day we found ourselves at the hardware store buying a dozen "no trespassing" signs.

"What we really need," I told my husband, "is a horse so I can patrol our ridge land."

"Or a dog," said our son, Jack. "A big dog."

"Could you two just help me find a staple gun?" he asked.

For the next two weeks, we discussed the merits of getting animals. I wanted a horse, my son wanted an American bulldog, and my husband wanted peace and quiet.

We needed animals, I reasoned. At a literary conference up in Chattanooga I'd attended right before moving down to Georgia, I'd heard one of the authors talking about Southerners and their animals in Southern literature. Since many of the stories took place in rural areas, and now we lived out in the country, we needed animals to fit in.

A few weeks later, we found ourselves at the breeders, Jack checking out a brindle litter of American bulldog pups and I petting a sweet dark mare the breeder just happened to have for sale. Meanwhile, a white puppy with a black eye patch kissed up to my husband. By our second month down in Ringgold, we were the proud owners of two pups and two horses.

BACK IN THE SADDLE

Georgia, 2007

When I moved back to the country, I thought I'd simply pick up where I'd left off 35 years ago with horses. Growing up I'd owned, ridden, and shown horses. Although I hadn't ridden much since I left home for college, I assumed getting back into, and on top of, horses would be second nature.

My plan was to find another version of Sunny, my favorite horse of long ago, a feisty Arabian–Quarter Horse stallion. This time I'd make "Sunny" a mare, hopefully a gentler version and perhaps even an older girl, like me. I'd only been in Georgia for a few months when I went to see a prospect. In the paddock, a shapely bay approached and nuzzled her head against me. She was 12, an Arabian–Quarter Horse cross with a long and sleek mane and tail. A mahogany bay, and darker than Sunny, she could have been his daughter, or granddaughter. Her name was "Fancy."

The day she was delivered in a trailer, she stepped off nervously and started flinging her head around. I took the lead rope and tried to calm her down, noticing in the process how she towered over me. She seemed higher strung than she was the day I met her, and as I led her along the road to the gate, I had to jog to keep up with her. I huffed and puffed in the June heat and wondered if I might have a heart attack before we ever made it to the pasture. (But what a way to die!)

A few days later after we had both calmed down, I bridled her with the new snaffle bridle I'd bought and planned to jump on and ride bareback as I had as a slim teenager. My husband, Steve, held the reins as I launched my size-14 body from the ground. I made it halfway up. Four times.

"Here, let me boost you," offered my husband. "You'll get your horse muscles back soon." After begrudgingly accepting his help, I sat happily atop her, my legs hugged around her soft body. We moved through the pasture, and I thought what a pleasure not to worry about her raring up and throwing me off as Sunny had in days gone by. By the creek, I pondered my good fortune. Lost in a reverie of déjà vu, I was shocked when I felt myself being tossed up in the air. I landed flat on my back onto hard ground, and lay there numb from the shock of falling off. She must have spooked at a turtle or a beaver in the creek. After the feeling returned to my back, and I was sure nothing was broken, I jumped up and ran after her, found her shivering about a quarter of a mile away. Mad at myself for falling off, I decided to get back on, proving to her and myself that I wasn't afraid. After, of course, I found my husband, so he could boost me up.

The next time I rode, and now that I knew Fancy sometimes spooked, I decided to use a saddle. I pulled out my 40-year-old English saddle and bought a new girth to fit Fancy's rounder belly. With my husband's help, I strapped on the saddle, put my foot in the stirrup, and began to mount—when the leather stirrup strap snapped out from under me. My husband caught me mid-air, on the way down. He assured me the leather had rotted and encouraged me to put away the old saddle that had worked so well four decades ago. He insisted I buy a new saddle—and a helmet.

Things were going smoothly, and I improvised when I couldn't remember what I'd done before. One blistering day, my son and I drove his car out into the field to check on my horse. When I couldn't find a fence post nearby to tie her up, I simply looped the lead rope over her neck and tied her to the car's door handle, so I could get the curry comb and feed from the trunk. While I was opening the trunk, she spooked. I felt the car rock, heard a loud snap, and looked up to see her bolting away across the field, red lead rope and car handle dragging behind. My son and I ran after her for the next 10 minutes, finally caught her in a remote corner of the field trembling. I grabbed the rope and calmed her down, but my son was inconsolable. The door handle was nowhere in sight. Thus, we ended up at the body shop paying $99 for a new door handle.

"What were you thinking?" my son asked.

"That never happened before," I answered.

Fancy seemed lonesome, so we bought another horse, Zip, a tall, older chestnut gelding with an attitude. On a whim one day when we hadn't brought the tack, my older sister Judy and I decided to ride bareback. I fashioned halters and lead ropes into hackamores, and my son boosted us up.

"Are you sure this is a good idea, Mom?" he asked. I cockily assured him it was—we'd been around horses all our lives—well, except for that 35-year gap. We headed off toward the creek. All was well until Zip bucked, not once, but twice. I watched as Judy flew up in slow motion, a look of horror on her face. She fell to the ground with a loud thud, causing Fancy to spook and jump up out from under me. We sat across from each other on the hard ground, and I looked at my sister, a distressed, 61-year-old woman. She wasn't 16 anymore. Neither was I.

"Are you alright?" I asked. She was, except for a stiff back and arm. I felt okay too unless you counted my sore lower back and bruised ego. I walked over to comfort Fancy, who looked as scared as we were. Zip? He grazed nonchalantly nearby, not a care in the world.

Getting back in the saddle wasn't at all what I expected. With her rounded body and gentle demeanor, my mare isn't really like the fiery stallion I once rode, and I am not the agile girl of my bareback days. When we canter along the same trails where I rode my first pony half a century ago, some things are the same—the sweet smell of grass, the rolling motion of the horse beneath me, the wind blowing through the horse's mane and my hair. In the melding of horse and rider, there is no past, no future, only the joy of the moment.

PASTORAL DIVERSIONS

Georgia, 2007

"What do you do for fun?" my California friends often ask. They refer, of course, to our life down in the Catoosa countryside.

"Plenty," I tell them. Thankfully, we don't have to drive too far for entertainment. A sultry Saturday late afternoon down in Woodstation finds us having a wild time down in our pasture.

Greeting me at the barn is what appears to be a blue-tailed snake. As I approach, the snake slithers, or darts, in between the old wooden planks that make up the barn walls. Seeing how fast this creature moves, I yell for my husband to come check it out. He goes into the barn and spots its neon blue tail—and little feet.

"Snakes don't have feet," he says. Turns out it's a lizard called a blue-tailed skink that can shed its tail when confronted by predators. But back to the task at hand: sowing our wild oats—err, grass seed.

A warm, gentle rain has left the air steamy and the ground moist, the perfect time to plant winter rye, according to Uncle Harry, who knows these types of things, having worked as a greens consultant on golf courses for many years. Although autumn officially began September 22, you wouldn't know it from the heat and humidity that insist on hanging on like cockleburs in a horse's tail.

Steve (with Bella the bulldog riding shotgun) drives our pickup while I, my sister, and my son ride in the truck bed with the sacks of seed and fertilizer. We toss handfuls of seed and fertilizer over the bare areas of the pasture and dirt road. As we sow, our mood is festive, despite sweat that runs down our foreheads and into our eyes. Perhaps it's because we know come winter, the horses will enjoy eating fresh green grass, but it's more likely it's because we are focusing on the task at hand. For the moment, we feel like farmers, something that comes naturally in our family. Grandma and Grandpa spent a lifetime in these very fields raising crops and animals and rearing children. Dipping our hands into seed buckets, swinging out our arms, flinging seed into air, and hearing the sound of seed scattering against the earth satisfy on some essential level and connect us to our agrarian roots.

The horses, by nature curious creatures, come over to check us out. As they watch us tossing the seed on the ground, I can almost read their minds. *Could that be oats?* they seem to say. They sniff at seed and fertilizer, then turn away.

After all the sowing is over, the fun continues. We spot cow bones, a rabbit, and a skunk with its tail held high. By the Little Chickamauga Creek, a white heron lifts off from its nest atop a tall tree. He wheels away into the dusky sky. In the nearby bottoms, we visit a meadow of purple, white, and gold wildflowers where migrating monarch butterflies flutter. Tossed on the creek bank, we see a pair of men's under shorts, red and medium-sized, left behind. Did someone go fishing and lose his pants? Did Santa go skinny dipping and get dressed too hastily? The possibilities are—endless.

Leaving behind pasture and critters on another fall evening, we head over to church for a wedding. Just down the road from our farm, Woodstation United Methodist Church is the heart of the community and has been there ever since I can remember. Although the church dates back to the mid or late 1830s when it was known as Bethel Methodist Episcopal Church, the current structure was built in 1947 on land given by my grandparents. The colorful stained-glass windows were given in honor, or memory, of members and those who lost their lives in World War II.

On this mild fall evening, the pews are filled with friends and family of an older couple who have come to re-marry each other. Glowing candles placed in the windowsills reflect the pastel shapes of the stained glass. The focus tonight is not so much on the couple but on gospel music provided by friends and family. As I listen to voices, guitar, and piano, I am amazed by the high quality of music here in my church, right here in this small community that is now my home. After everyone has played or sung, the couple exchanges vows. The celebration continues with cake and fellowship downstairs.

Afterwards, we drive home, sated with music and cake. I reflect on our good fortune in finding fun so close by, yet I am wistful the evening has come to an end.

Passing by our barn, I console myself by thinking of all the surprises yet to come in our pasture. Winter rye will soon sprout up, and the horses' coats will thicken in the coming weeks. As we head into cooler weather, rabbits, skunks, cardinals, and other wildlife will cross our paths. If confronted by a predator, the blue-tailed skink will no doubt lose his tail. And who knows? Maybe we'll spot Santa down at the creek, coming back to claim those red shorts.

WEATHERING OUR MOVE

No matter how long the winter, spring is sure to follow.

—Proverb

Georgia, 2007

"Do you realize you're leaving paradise?" my friend asked. We were standing on the bluffs above the Pacific Ocean on a clear day in February both wearing shorts and T-shirts. I had taken a break from packing up our house for our move from Southern California to Georgia.

"It can't be that bad," I said. "I like having four seasons. And besides, remember I grew up down there." She shook her head.

"Don't say I didn't warn you," she said.

It wasn't that I hadn't thought of the weather. Steve and I had planned our move for springtime when temperatures would be what we were accustomed to; the air would be warm and welcoming.

In April 2007, we arrived at our new home to weather that seemed the same as what we'd left, even sunnier. Carrying in boxes from the moving van, I remarked that I'd have to unpack my summer wardrobe first. It was so warm that I would need to change into shorts and sandals. A few days later, my husband and I stood on our back porch and surveyed our new yard, which was bordered by woods. We saw the white blooms of a slender dogwood tree peeking through the abundant branches of the pines and hardwoods.

"Just in time for Easter," I said. "With this warm weather, it's really not that different from California," I said.

"Just wait till next winter," he said.

We didn't have to wait at all. On Easter morning we woke up to temperatures in the teens. Overnight, the fragile dogwood blossoms had frozen. I dug around in the closet and pulled out a heavy coat I'd not worn in 20 years. Bundled up, I still shivered as we walked into church. Steve whispered to me, "Dorothy, we're not in Kansas anymore." Definitely not Kansas, but maybe Alaska.

The locals assured us this was unusual—the coldest Easter they remembered. Some called the cold snap a "dogwood winter." Plants and trees turned dark, and many crops were ruined.

Soon, the weather got back on track with a warming trend. When we went to pick out a puppy at the kennel, I remarked on the lovely weather. The dog breeder, also a California transplant, warned us.

"In the summer you'll pray for winter, and in the winter, you'll pray for summer," he said. My husband laughed. It was May and perfect weather.

By the sweltering days of August, I longed for the deep freeze of Easter. Every time I walked the dog or tended to the horses, I had to change out of my sweat-drenched clothes. Soon, I was washing two loads a day of laundry and wondering why we'd moved in the first place.

Thankfully, fall arrived along with mold spores that triggered allergies, followed by a cold and gloomy winter that brought new challenges. I learned how hard it is to unlatch a gate when your fingers are frozen to the metal chain and how many days of overcast gray skies it takes to make one consider jumping on a plane and heading for the Caribbean. Winter storms brought rumbling thunder that shook our house and felt like small earthquakes, and lightning hit our house, burning out several pieces of electronic equipment. The rough weather caused many of our backyard slender pines to bend or fall. Heavy downpours turned our barn road into a sucking mud pit. I learned how to get my car unstuck from the mud—three times.

Finally, after what seemed like an eternity had passed, spring brought warmer weather. As Easter approached, I strolled around in our backyard, remembering our first Easter when the cold snap had frozen flowers in bloom. Looking toward our woods, I spotted the white-notched flowers of dogwood down low to the ground. I walked over and leaned down for a closer look. The dogwood tree was sideways, parallel to the ground, probably knocked down by a winter storm. Its trunk was buried by a pile of felled trees. This dogwood tree looked like it should be dead, not in bloom.

I broke off a branch of abundant white flowers. In our kitchen, I showed my son the blossoms and told him about the felled tree that had produced them.

"Does the tree still have its roots?" Jack asked. I had not actually been able to see the base of the dogwood's trunk.

"It has to be rooted," I said. "Otherwise, it couldn't grow, could it?" I filled a slim blue glass vase with water, put in the branch of blossoms, and set the arrangement atop the dining room table. The notched petals held fast to the thin, strong branches. I admired its heartiness, its ability to flourish despite being knocked down to the ground.

Getting used to this climate has been difficult, and each season brings new challenges. When I feel discouraged, I try to remember the sight of that hearty dogwood that bloomed on our first anniversary of living in Georgia. Although knocked down by bad weather, the dogwood tree somehow managed to stay rooted and thus was able to blossom.

GOING TO TOWN

"My momma always said, 'Life is like a box of chocolates. You never know what you're gonna get.'"—Forrest Gump

Georgia, 2009

It's a fine spring morning in the country, the kind of day where you want to sit on the porch and listen to the birds sing or take a walk in a field of daffodils. The day should be full of possibilities, not responsibilities such as going to work or driving to town on business to sit indoors in some stuffy office. Like a kid with spring fever, I'd rather stay outdoors and play. Although I'm not happy about it, Steve and I climb into our pick-up truck and head downtown for what hopefully will be a short business meeting.

As soon as we turn onto Nashville Street, I can see on this Friday I'm not the only one with spring fever. On the side of the road, several dozen children sit along the curb with their teachers hovering close behind. The youngsters look eagerly toward the street.

"Did you see those kids' faces?" I ask Steve. "They all look excited, like something's about to happen."

"Maybe they're going on a field trip and they're waiting for the bus to pick them up," Steve speculates. He is probably right, and the day is perfect for a field trip. Not too warm, and a little overcast.

We find a parking spot right on Nashville in the center of town and enter a stylishly decorated office. A friendly receptionist tells us that they are running behind, and we are welcome to take a seat in the conference room. Spying an empty bench outside, I ask if we can wait there. It's just too nice a day to stay inside. Sure, she says, and we head outside.

Sitting on the bench, we discuss just how long we might have to wait till our meeting begins. I remark to Steve that it's odd to have a free moment to simply sit on a bench and watch the world go by. The longer we wait on that bench, time seems to slow down, and I began to feel like Forrest Gump waiting for the bus in the town square. Steve notices there's not much traffic, and in fact, no cars at all. Then I think I hear music in the air.

"What was that?" I ask Steve.

"Sounds like a band," he says. I jump up from the bench and stare down Nashville Street to see where it's coming from. I am greeted with the sight of an aqua-colored Special Olympics banner, the sheriff and fire department, and clowns. Soon, a convertible with waving students follows, and then a band dressed in yellow Special Olympics t-shirts playing "Glory, Glory." I am impressed with their playing of this familiar tune, and I wonder if this is the Ringgold High band. A gentleman escorting them waves at us. I wave back, recognizing him as the director of the Ringgold High School band. High-stepping girls twirling batons pass, and the music continues with the Lakeview-Fort Oglethorpe marching band dressed in red Special Olympics t-shirts and playing "Hail to Georgia." Gentlemen wearing red fezzes motor past in miniature Model T's. It's the Shriners' Tin Lizzies unit, and they seem to be having the most fun of all.

Now I'm excited and caught up in the moment. Floats with smiling, waving students and their teachers pass. I wave back. I spot other familiar faces, a friend and her son, waving from their spot with the Lakeview-Fort Oglethorpe High School group. I wave back and am rewarded with a shower of plastic-wrapped hard candy tossed my way. From the distance, I hear the strains of "Georgia on My Mind," and I find myself singing the words that have always made me homesick for the pine trees and pastures of Northwest Georgia.

"Georgia, Georgia, the whole day through…"

Even though it's a fine spring day out in the country, I suddenly am aware I'd rather be no place else at the moment but right here in the center of Ringgold, my new hometown, watching this parade of special athletes and volunteers. On a spring day, it doesn't get any better than baton twirlers, marching bands, and free candy.

OKRA ODYSSEY

California, Early 2000s

Once I moved back to the South, finding good fresh okra was much easier than it was when I lived out West. Out there, the neighborhood stores often carried rusty-looking, wilted okra, and at a high price, or oversized dry and stringy pods. So, when I woke up one sunny California morning craving okra, I set out to find a mess of the fresh, earthy-smelling pods that have always reminded me of Grandma and home.

After checking supermarkets, I tried my luck at the farmer's market set up in a roped off street in the middle of the town where I lived. Wearing sturdy pink tennis shoes and an optimistic attitude, I arrived fairly early at the rows of outdoor stalls ahead of the crowds, or so I thought. Hurrying past bouquets of Gerbera daisies and roses, sample slices of peaches and apples, I scanned the tables for green things. Broccoli, Brussels sprouts, green beans, and lettuce. Tucked between a box of Bok choy and collards, there was a box of okra large enough to feed an army, or my competition, a white-haired man who was standing with his hands already buried deep in the cool pods.

He scooped a generous handful of okra into his bag. His accomplice, or wife, I imagined, stood next to him supervising.

"Only the smaller ones, honey," she said. I moved closer.

"They are the most tender, aren't they?" I chimed in. "How do you cook them?" I asked. I was hankering to get my hands into that bin, but I held back.

"In a gumbo," the man replied in a thick southern accent.

"Are y'all from the South, too?" I asked.

"From near Charleston," the man answered. "My family settled there 200 years ago." Shoot, my Durant ancestors were probably there to greet him, I thought, but didn't say. No point in alienating him, especially since he was at Ground Zero, okra-wise.

"Are you from the South?" his wife asked. "I hear an accent."

"Georgia and Tennessee," I answered. Suddenly, and in true Southern gentleman fashion, the husband moved aside slightly, making room for me to join him at the okra bin. God love him. I plunged my hands into the okra, let my fingers rummage through all those pods, feeling for the tiniest of them while staying on my side of the box, of course. The first rule of okra etiquette is not to take all the best pods, especially when there's another Southerner in the picture.

"How do you prepare yours?" his wife asked. I described my Georgia grandma's recipe for fried okra where the okra is sliced into pinwheels, dipped in a cornbread mix, and fried for a very long time—until it's very brown and crisp or until you can't stand the wonderful smell anymore and are forced to serve it up at once.

"And what about your stew? Do you use them whole, or sliced?" I asked.

"Sliced," he said. "Helps to thicken the stew."

"I see," I said. We soon found ourselves pointing out the smallest pods to one another, taking our time even though a line was beginning to form. After each of us had taken our fair share (or perhaps a wee bit more in my case) we shook hands.

"Nice talking with both of you," I said.

"Likewise," he answered. His wife nodded and smiled, and we all moved away from the okra area to let the others have a shot.

Back at home, over plates of crisp, browned fried okra, I told my family about my quest to find a good batch of okra and about meeting the other Southerners. And the following Sunday, I woke up early, got dressed, and traveled back to the farmers' market and the okra bin. Realizing that the process is almost more fun than the result, I took my time picking okra and struck up conversations with other okra lovers. Several were from the South, and several were from other countries. All generously shared tips on preparing okra.

By summer's end, I'd eaten stewed okra, steamed okra, fried okra, and even dried okra! I'd chalked up a dozen visits to the farmers' market in search of the perfect pods. I'd picked through hundreds of pods and visited with people with Southern accents and people with foreign accents. Because of okra, that summer I met people from all over the world.

Now that I live down South, I can find quality okra in abundance at local grocery stores or farm stands. If I'm lucky,

Aunt Barbara will phone and tell me to come pick some from her garden. In the heat of the summer, I frequent produce stands that dot the countryside. One blistering day when I pulled up to a stand in Ringgold and started to climb out of my car, the produce fellow waved me away and told me to come back later. He pointed to a black and white visitor. A skunk stood in the cool shade under the shelves holding baskets of tomatoes and squash!

When I find myself on the road this summer and missing the South, I'll look for the fuzzy pods in stores, or stop and visit a produce stand. No matter where I travel, when I'm at an okra bin, I feel right at home. That is, of course, if a skunk doesn't beat me to it.

A THORNY ISSUE

"In this world nothing can be said to be certain, except death and taxes." —Benjamin Franklin

Georgia, 2009

As if death and taxes aren't bad enough, a third thing should be added to the list: cockleburs. Our first summer down here in Georgia, my family and I found ourselves caught up in an endless task of plucking out the clingy globes from the horses' manes and tails and later, back at home, from our pants and socks.

As we walked through the pasture, I observed the life cycles and types of burs. A low-to-the-ground type started off looking like collard greens and later bore cute little mini-pods that turned into small clusters of cockleburs. These collard-type burs stuck to the horses in clumps and were hard to remove, so difficult that one time I had to cut off most of my mare's mane and tail. A second type of bur, which I call "the evil cousin," has lacier leaves and thorns and grows into barrel-shaped burs with deceptive lovely lavender flowers sprouting off their tops. There, bumble bees like to visit. Don't let that flower fool you—the bur underneath has sharp, hard needles that catch onto animals and people, and if touched can make you bleed. The lavender flower later morphs into white feathers that blow in the wind. So goes the life cycle of the cocklebur …

Talking with farmer friends, I find out that poison might be the answer to our "bur problem." At a local feed store, I purchase a giant-sized container and borrow a sprayer from my sister. But when I read the label and see all the precautions, I cringe. If it's so toxic, what's to prevent it from hurting the horses, rabbits, or us? So, we continue to battle the burs the old-fashioned way: by hand.

This summer, when the dreaded burs start to sprout up, so does my killer instinct. Walking through the pasture spotting the plants, I bend over, gripping my hands around their throats—stems—and yank up hard. After a few days of rain, I find this approach works on the little ones. But on the big plants, I must use two hands and pull back hard. One specimen, two feet tall, sticks to the earth like a cocklebur to horse's tail. It won't budge. I tug, and tug, and finally rip it out of the earth with such great force that I almost fall back onto the ground. On the really tall, stubborn ones, I can't get them pulled up, so I simply rip off their stems at ground level, having no idea whether or not it will work. Some say you have to get the roots, too. But I figure if I can kill before the pods come out, the burs can't reproduce. I hope.

As summer days progress, burs pop up everywhere like jack rabbits. I recruit a neighbor girl to pull, or dig up, the plants at 50 cents a pop. Although she works hard, and succeeds in removing 70 of them, more seem to spring up overnight. They are prolific and annoying.

When a friend from California visits, we drive around the pasture in my Volvo wagon, and I point out some of the dreaded plants. Noting the artichoke-type pods erupting, Anne innocently asks, "Are you sure that's not an artichoke?"

"Artichoke, smartichoke!" I reply. "Let's kill those suckers!" I push down hard on the gas pedal, and we bounce around the field bush using the Volvo's bumper and undercarriage to whack them down.

"I never knew you were like this," she says.

"Like what?" I ask as I mow down another of the lavender-topped plants.

"So wild," she says.

"I hate them!" I reply and give a Rebel yell as we drive over several more plants. She laughs and joins in the fun. She begins coaching me.

"Get that one!" she says, "over there." As much fun as we have, in my rear-view mirror I see the plants spring right back up. A fun, but futile, exercise.

A few days later in the pasture, seeing the prickly plants everywhere we turn, my husband Steve pulls out the swing blade and gets tough. We work as a team against our arch enemies: I point, he cuts. One Saturday, an hour into the battle after he has chopped down a plant taller than he, Steve looks down to see the wooden handle has split in two. Reluctantly, we call it a day, but not for long. He promises to fix the swing blade and soon continue the battle.

I've even thought of other approaches such as purchasing three or four swing blades and convincing family and friends that the swinging action is great upper body exercise and good practice for their golf swing. I could invite them over for a cocklebur party and give prizes to the one who chops down the most plants. It worked for Tom Sawyer and his fence, didn't it?

Until I can find some takers, I'm left to face my bur problem on a daily basis. Like a spy researching the enemy, I go online to learn more about the invaders that have taken over our fields. If eaten, cocklebur seedlings and seeds can be poisonous to horses. The collard-type plant might be burdock, and the lacey barrel type is lavender thistle. Burdock is said to have medicinal uses, and cockleburs inspired a Swiss hiker to invent a new fastener. In the 1940s, George de Mestral walked his dog in the woods and came home to pull off, and study, cockleburs to see how they worked. He then created Velcro.

I'm glad some folks have found good use for these sticky monsters, but down here in the country, who needs cockleburs? And why were these thorny annoyances created in the first place? Only God knows. Next time I'm out in the field I'll stop and ask one of the bumble bees.

SOUTHERN SPEAK

Georgia, 2008

Hi, baby doll. How y'all been sugar? I still can't get used to these terms of endearment, but you know when folks refer to me with these sweet words in my new home, I feel good.

When I first landed in Georgia, I felt squeamish with these too familiar, over-the-top endearments. After all, I'd only met the woman uttering them in the last 30 seconds, and the only person who regularly called me "baby" has been dead for 20 years. But after living in the South for a few months, with lingering homesickness for my California friends, I found myself popping into the places where "sugar baby" and "baby doll" are uttered in sincerity to each valued customer. After six months in the South, I found myself anticipating the nicknames I'm called by complete strangers.

The shower of endearments left me feeling loved and wanted. Who knew an outing to the Dollar Store could leave me feeling as pampered and cared for as a trip to a Beverly Hills day spa? Like a spoiled child, I now find myself looking forward to my next trip to Ringgold and these terms of endearment, even though as I exit the store, I can hear the person in line after me being treated the same way. I am not special, am I? Or maybe we are all special? I'd like to think.

On a recent visit to California, linguistic differences were apparent. No one calls me baby doll, or honey, and dining out, the server (always an aspiring actor) introduces himself with a smile and an overly cheerful recitation of today's low-fat special. I am not asked "rolls or cornbread" or what type of bread I want, and in fact, no bread is brought to the table. Perhaps the waiter assumes that, like two million others in L.A. I'm on a diet. Or perhaps by not bringing bread he's implying I should be? Perish the thought … When I inquire about bread, I am informed that it doesn't come with my meal, and if I want it, I'll have to pay extra. I'll skip, thank you. When the waiter asks me what I want to drink, I say, "Iced tea, unsweet" and am given a perplexing look. Out in California, iced tea is served with no sugar, and folks are expected to doctor it up themselves. My husband pipes up,

"We're living in the South now." Oh, so that would account for any strange behavior, the waiter seems to say with his smile.

There are other important linguistic considerations. Down South I can be expected to be called "ma'am," even by folks older than I am. I finally figured out that being called "ma'am" didn't necessarily mean I am old (although one could argue that point). Down here, being called "ma'am" is a term of respect. Whereas "baby doll" and "honey" are supposed to make me feel good, "ma'am" makes me feel respected and honored. When someone says "ma'am" I feel as though there's hope for our civilization. After all, the Queen of England was addressed as "ma'am." But here in Georgia, when you hear "ma'am" it can be a good thing, or a bad thing, depending on the tone in which it's said and the context. For example, if you've been pulled over by the sheriff and he asks, "Ma'am, is there a fire somewhere?" as he writes you a ticket, this is not the same as "Yes, ma'am" the server says when you ask for a container to take home the extra rolls or cornbread.

"Y'all" is similar to "you guys" which can mean just one person, or the entire gang as I found out once when I said, "Why don't y'all come over?" and six guests showed up.

Down here, using the word "y'all" can be risky, especially when food is involved. You can be sure when you say, "y'all come on over for dinner" the invitee thinks you mean him or her, spouse, children, grandkids, and coon dogs. The only way to get around this is to point at the person as you say "y'all" adding, "I'll set an extra place for you." To be safe, you might want to add that, due to the drought, crop failures, and so on, you have just enough extra beans and cornbread to feed one extra person nicely.

Speaking of vegetables, there's nothing better than to have a neighbor give you a "mess of beans" or a "mess of okra." Out in California, the only "mess" I received for free was the canine variety, stuck to the bottom of my sole after visiting the dog park. Down here in the South, "a mess" is not a definite amount but somehow always turns out to be just the right amount to feed a family, at least when "y'all" doesn't show up. But if some unexpected guests show up, and all you have is a "mess of beans," you can always serve some "sweet or unsweet" and smile. Whether you serve "rolls or cornbread," just remember everything seems to taste better when served up with a little "Honey" and "Sugar."

NIGHT VISITOR

"Was it a vision or a waking dream?" —John Keats

Georgia, 2009

One cold winter's night I sat in the kitchen flipping through a magazine. Suddenly I spotted something in my peripheral vision. A dark object seemed to zip across past my left eye. A giant beetle? A hallucination? Whatever it was, maybe the dog had seen it too.

"Bella?" I called. My American bulldog's white head bobbed up from clear across the room. She had slept through the entire incident—or perceived incident. Had I imagined I'd seen something? Perhaps the cold, dark and long days of winter out here in the Georgia countryside were starting to get to me.

Then I saw it again. A fat black mouse scurrying right across the hardwood floor, headed toward the kitchen cabinet. I jumped up and tried to follow, but the little critter disappeared into nowhere. I moved the trash can, searched the baseboards looking for cracks or secret holes where the mouse might have escaped. Nothing.

"Steve?" I called up the stairs for my husband. "I just saw a mouse."

"You shouldn't leave the garage door open," he replied. "I've been telling you guys to keep the doors shut." It was true. For many years, I've had the bad habit of leaving the door to the inside of the house open while unloading things from the car. One rainy, foggy California night, I unloaded the car through an open door, only to later walk into the bathroom to find myself in a standoff with an angry possum.

"No telling how many more mice there are," Steve said. "They carry diseases. You'll have to get some traps."

"Tomorrow," I answered. It was late and the stores were closed. Besides, I hoped there was something a little more humane than a trap. I turned to the internet.

Other than pest control companies and the usual traps, what caught my eye was a new method that promised to capture the mouse unharmed. You get a trash can 12 inches or deeper. Place a plastic liner inside and put something sweet in the bottom, such as cereal or raisins. While you sleep, the mouse is supposed to smell the food, then jump from the counter into the trash can where he will remain stuck and unable to climb out. The next morning you simply take out the trash—and mouse—and dump into the yard. The whole plan sounded smart and reminded me of those diving horses of Atlantic City I had heard about but never saw. The horse was taken to a high tower, a rider climbed aboard, and the pair jumped off into a tank of water far below. People paid to see the performance.

This mouse in the trash can approach sounded like such an adventure that maybe the mouse in our house would actually enjoy himself. Heck, he might even bring along the whole family for a night of trash jumping. A bungee jumping outing, mouse-style.

I rounded up the trash can, lined it with plastic, and carefully selected one of my favorite honey and almond cereals. I scooted the can up to the counter and tiptoed off to bed. I listened for a long time and fell asleep thinking about what would happen in my kitchen while I slumbered.

The next morning, I rushed in to look for the mouse, or mice, so I could begin the relocation project. In the can, I spotted a banana peel and some paper towels. Perhaps the entire herd of mice had dragged the banana along behind them as they dove into the can? Or attempted to use the paper towel pieces as parachutes? Bending over the can, I used a large plastic spoon to push aside the banana peel. Not a single mouse in sight.

Further questioning the usual suspects, my husband, and son, revealed that both had forgotten about the mouse-jumping-into-trash-can scheme and had thrown in the usual garbage. And apparently, the mice have not heard about the fun night of adventure planned for them. So, I went to Plan B, off to the hardware to purchase some traps, the spring-loaded type guaranteed not to be much fun for either mouse or me.

Back at home, Steve set the traps out near the trash cans (the regular one and the mouse-jumping can) just in case. The next morning, we expected to find a captured mouse either in the can or the traps. Not a single one showed up.

On the third mouse-less day, we decided that the mouse had simply been passing through, a traveling mouse on his way somewhere else. I was reaching up to grab some tea bags when I heard a scratching noise from the cabinets below. I squatted down and listened to the sound of tiny claws doing something in my food storage bin. It didn't sound like just one mouse but more like a mother and her babies. Was she building a nest?

We relocated the traps to the cabinets where the sounds came from and waited. Every morning, I checked the traps, but no mice.

Several weeks passed, and I heard no more scratching noises or scurrying in the cabinets. I'm not sure where the mouse, or mice family, went. While I'm glad I didn't have to deal with finding a mouse caught in a spring-loaded trap, I sure would have liked to have been around to see that mouse swan dive into that trash can.

CHANGING HORSES

"You gotta know when to hold 'em, know when to fold 'em,

know when to walk away and know when to run."

—Kenny Rogers

Georgia, 2010

At first he seemed so nice. He was tall, good-looking, and charming, seemingly a gentleman. But that was in the riding ring where he had spent the last dozen years teaching youngsters to ride.

Once our new chestnut gelding arrived at our farm, he changed. The formerly well-behaved Quarter Horse soon turned into a pawing, kicking, jumping, and bucking machine. Frustrated, we consulted the local horse whisperer who suggested we teach this bad boy a lesson by tying him with a sturdy rope to a tree for an entire day. We tied "Buck" up to the tree with a strong rope using a leather halter. Within five minutes he'd snapped the rope and galloped away to find Fancy, our mare, er, I mean *his* mare.

Maybe she was the problem. Maybe he was trying to show off for the mare, or maybe he couldn't stand being separated from her, even for a second. We decided we'd only ride them together. We saddled up both horses and headed off into the pasture. Things went smoothly, for about five minutes, until Mr. Buck started "crow-hopping," a euphemism for mild bucking, unless you're the one getting tossed around in the saddle. Then it's just plain bucking.

We wanted it to work, so we kept at it. My husband put in hours of groundwork, leading and lunging. Buck fought back with his size—15 ½ hands high—coming in close trying, but failing, to intimidate my husband. When corrected, Buck would behave for a day, or two, then quickly return to his bullying ways. No one wanted to ride him, but we hated to give up. Buck had cost us a pretty penny, and he came from good bloodlines. We worked with him for months and experimented with various types of tack. Surely it was us, we thought, or something we were doing.

Once again, we called in the horse whisperer, and he came over to work with Mr. Buck. He led and lunged him in the ring. After a few hours of trying to bring Mr. Buck into line, the horse whisperer gave his recommendation. Get rid of the horse.

We didn't want to sell him and pass along a "lemon," so we decided to offer him for free to our friend, who was an experienced horseman and who had expressed an interest. I knew he would be able to handle Buck. After all, he had ridden in rodeos.

Still, when the day came for our parting, and Buck was loaded into the trailer, I couldn't help feeling sad as it pulled away. Buck craned his long neck to get a final glimpse of Fancy as the trailer pulled out of the gate. Buck neighed plaintively, and constantly, as the trailer drove off and out of sight. Guilt tugged at my heart. Poor Buck was never to see our, *his,* mare again. I was such a bad owner. But then Steve spoke.

"You would have felt worse if he'd hurt someone," he said. And he was right.

A few weeks later we find ourselves wishing for another horse, a companion for our mare. We travel up to the Chattanooga Stock Yard to the Friday night auction. There we find a barn full of prospects.

The animals look confused or depressed. "Why did I land here?" they seem to ask with their questioning eyes. Perhaps the black walking horse with ears laid back regrets bucking off his previous owner. On the catwalk above the stalls, potential buyers voice their opinions of the horses. Young boys ride the prospects up and down the center aisle constantly, a parade of horseflesh. As I duck into a stall to pet a young, shy bay, I think about "Black Beauty" of the classic tale and her many owners. Horse-wise, nothing has really changed much. Horses are at the whims of their owners. I think of Buck, but I know he's in better hands, and at least he's not at the auction.

I have heard that getting a horse at the auction can be risky, but we are prepared. To be on the safe side, we have brought along two horse expert friends to share their opinions. When I spot a red gelding with a sweet face, I bring over my experts. After checking his legs, hooves, and mouth, both declare he is sound. I take a test ride and find him easily manageable, and surprisingly cooperative. I don't want to get off.

Soon, we find ourselves in the stands above the auction arena. The auctioneer's chant brings in only low bids for most of the horses. It's winter, feed is high, and they sell for little money. Until "Red" is brought out. The crowd murmurs its approval as he's led around the ring, and the bidding begins. One hundred, I raise my hand. One twenty. One fifty, I raise my hand.

"Hold off," Steve whispers.

"I want this horse!" I whisper back. Soon, we are up to three seventy-five, and then my hand shoots up.

"Four hundred," I yell.

"Going once, going twice, sold to the lady for four hundred," the auctioneer declares. The red, seemingly gentle gelding now belongs to me, the lady in the stands who has decided to take a gamble on a new horse.

BARN BUDDY

Georgia, 2013

One day my dog Bella and I headed out to the pasture to do horse chores. Fancy, my foundered mare, was once again penned up and requiring extra care. I was mentally planning out chores and scanning the horizon for my other two horses when I heard a soft mewing.

The day before, neighbors had been haying the next field over. My first thought was that a feral mama cat had transported her baby to safety—into the shed where I keep Fancy. "Kitty, kitty," I called. A black and brown kitten shyly peeked out from behind a briar patch. I rummaged around in my belt pack and found the only food I had—a saltine cracker. Bella, my American bulldog, growled as she watched the kitten gobbling up cracker bits.

The cat hissed. Bella lunged. The cat darted up a nearby tree.

I scolded Bella, then went about doing my barn business, which involves a lot of shoveling and rolling of a wheelbarrow. (Why I don't already have biceps like a bodybuilder is another story). As I worked, I contemplated the poor, motherless, and now treed little kitty. I figured her mama would soon come to collect her, and they would go away to live happily ever after—somewhere else.

Cats are titillating creatures. They also trigger my allergies. Thus, taking this lost and mewing creature into my home was not an option. Besides, Bella hates cats. And since Bella is the ruler in our home, whatever she wants, she gets.

Later that day, I returned to the pasture. As I walked through high grass toward the paddock area, I listened for sounds of mewing. Nothing. The cat was gone. I was relieved. Clanging open the round pen gate, I poured feed into the horses' buckets. Through their munching noises, I heard the faint sound of mewing. I left the horses to follow the sound, Bella on my heels.

The mewing seemed to come from a tall tree near the watering troughs. I looked up—way up—and saw a blur of black and brown fur perpendicular to the gray bark. The kitty was safely perched yet seemed to want my attention. I talked to her, and she mewed back. Bella stood motionless, ready to pounce.

"I'll come back tomorrow and bring you food," I told her.

After a restless night worrying about the new kitten, I woke up early, grabbed a handful of Bella's dry food, and headed out. I found the cat waiting by the side of the paddock area, mewing loudly for the food I'd promised. I poured some on the ground. She gobbled it up.

From Bella's point of view, I was acting strangely. I was commiserating with the enemy, and in fact feeding it. And I was in danger! This purring and slinky creature could claw me at any moment. She had to get rid of the threat. She pounced. Kitty drew up, hissed, and lashed out with her claws, bolted for the nearest pine tree. She shot up. Way up. Twenty feet or more. Bella charged through the briar patch and stood barking at the tree.

"Bad dog. Don't hurt the kitty!" I ordered.

Bella glanced back at me and seemed to say, "What? Have you gone nuts? I finally got her treed, did my job, and you're mad at me?"

"She's a baby," I told Bella. Bella backed off a bit, although I could see by her baffled expression that she had her reservations. I ordered her to the car and left her there. I tried to coax the kitty down. The branches she might descend on were widely spaced. No way could she get down alone. Was it time to call the fire department? And down here, do they show up for this type of emergency? Worst of all, would I have to pay for it? I decided to leave the cat be for the night. At least a pack of coyotes wouldn't get her.

The next day Bella and I returned, Bella wearing a collar and leash and I carrying a dish and a handful of dried cat food. Anticipating their oats, the horses neighed in greeting. Louder still was the insistent mewing from the briar patch by the tree.

"Just a minute, horses," I snapped. I tied Bella to the fence and walked over to a spot near the briar patch, set down the dish, and poured out the feed. The cat weaved and purred her way over. She sniffed the food and started eating. I stroked her back while she feasted. I heard a low growl.

"Bella, it's alright. Can't you see she's starving?" Bella was not happy with this turn of events. Neither were the three hungry horses. They were accustomed to being the first served.

Days of kitty feeding turned into weeks. Using an inner discipline I never knew she had, Bella slowly began to leave the cat be.

Prior to the kitty's arrival, Fancy passed long hours alone in the shed in boredom, but now she has company. In fact, I named the kitty "Amie," French for friend. At night, Amie sleeps in the hay near the horse. I've seen the evidence, indentations in the hay shaped like a bird's nest.

As for me, I am adjusting to having another mouth to feed and other expenses. When Amie grew to her "cattin' around" age, I had her spayed. The last thing I need is more little ones.

I have finally figured out my job description. I am house mother to a fraternity of animals. I am the bearer of feed, the settler of disputes amongst the animals.

All of which is fine, except this house mother has to also come up with the money to feed her growing band of animals. Three horses, a large dog, and one tortoise shell cat. For now, membership to this pastoral fraternity is closed. At least that's what Bella says.

A GOOD AND GENTLE HORSE

Georgia, 2010

"She's a good, gentle horse," my friend said, describing one he knew was available. I was skeptical. Admittedly, I haven't had the best of luck with horses since moving to Georgia, but I wanted to add another to our pair. When I found out the horse was free, I had to jump in the car and drive down to the next county to meet her. Allegedly, this mare would come right up to you in the pasture and willingly drop her head right into a halter, no carrot necessary.

When we pulled up by the barn, I immediately spotted her among the small herd in the nearby pasture. She was the curious one that turned her head to look at us with dark, doe-like eyes. Slender and brown with a scooped nose, she looked part Arabian—until I saw her long ears. With those mule-like ears, I was afraid she might be stubborn. When I climbed on for a test ride in the riding arena, she was cooperative and moved slowly, but willingly. More importantly, she didn't try to buck me off.

"Why are you giving her away?" I asked her owner. The woman explained that her family was moving off their farm into a home with no room for horses. In fact, they were giving away several of their horses, but after my recent experiences with bucking horses, all I wanted was one gentle horse.

"If you'll let me have her, I'll take good care of her," I promised. "We spoil our horses," a huge understatement if there ever was one. Our horses are nothing if not pampered. A week later, the owner called to say I could have the mare, and a friend with a trailer helped me pick her up to bring her back to Woodstation.

Arriving at our farm, the new mare was showered with attention from our man-in-charge, Sunny, a feisty sorrel gelding. Since Sunny and our mare Fancy are like an old married couple, the new, younger female's arrival upset the apple cart. Sunny found the new mare so alluring that he abandoned Fancy and ran into the fields with his new love.

Despite her cavorting around with Sunny, the new mare was quick to leave him and run right over when we humans appeared. She would lower her head so she could be haltered and stretch out her legs as though posing for a photo shoot. When offered an apple or carrot, she would gingerly brush her lips against my palm, being careful not to bite the hand that fed her.

Noting her svelte look and refined ways, my husband dubbed her "Moneypenny" after the secretary featured in the James Bond movies. If Fancy had been in charge of names, the new mare would have been called "Trouble." Even seeing Moneypenny made Fancy lay back her ears. Poor Fancy, the first horse I'd bought when I moved here, quickly became the odd horse out. Pretty-faced Moneypenny became the dominant mare. Sunny? He was still the man in charge, herding the girls around the pasture in a most authoritative manner except when it came to electric fences. Then he hung back and let the girls go first, watching as they got zapped. Quite the gentleman, that Sunny.

For the first several months, Moneypenny enjoyed grazing our pasture and gained weight. She was a joy to ride, so easy to handle that children could ride her without an adult leading. More importantly, my sister Judy could ride her without fear and one day announced, "Finally a horse I can hang onto" as she trotted along.

Fresh spring grass brought stomach troubles to our new mare. Instead of trotting, she had the trots. The vet became a frequent visitor, and we tried pills, potions, changing feed, supplements, and wormers. Soon our barn was a pharmacopeia. Nothing really worked for long, and as her stomach woes worsened, she lost weight. We called in another vet for a second opinion, and he admitted he was stumped. As she lost weight, she weakened. She held her head low all the time and took halting steps. Nevertheless, she always came to us willingly, offering her delicate face for petting. After seven months of illness, she was 400 lbs. underweight, too weak to make it through the winter.

On a misty autumn day, she left us. We buried her in a spot near a tree where she had enjoyed grazing during the nine months she spent with us. For a day or two, Sunny kept searching for her, then settled into calm acceptance that one of his mares was gone. Not surprisingly, Fancy did not seem terribly upset at Moneypenny's absence.

But we were. We missed Moneypenny ambling toward us, always happy to see us. We missed her dear and delicate face, her big doe eyes, her inquisitive lips nibbling at our pockets in search of carrots. The loss of this horse, the sweetest I had ever known, hurt.

For now, I am going to love my two healthy horses. It may be a while before I take on another horse, free or otherwise.

From this gift horse, I learned that a horse's true value cannot be measured in dollars, only in emotion. A good and gentle horse will always own a piece of your heart.

BARN LIFE

Georgia, 2008

Our barn is probably at least 100 years old and looks its age. It sits lower on one side than the other and seems to be slowly settling into its final resting place—the rich brown earth that lies beneath. Although we have made patchwork repairs, the many spaces between boards make the barn well-ventilated for visiting critters. In addition to the blue skink (a type of lizard) we once encountered, I've seen mice and barn swallows inside the barn. Formerly used for hay storage, the creaky loft is home to feral cats that prey upon baby swallows who live in a nest built into a cross beam. Sometimes the hungry loft cats thrust their paws down through the ceiling cracks right into the swallows' nest to grab a tasty snack, leaving behind an empty nest and an array of feathers scattered on the barn floor.

One sweltering day we arrived at the barn to tend to the horses and found hornets swarming the side shed where hay bales are stored. Steve and Jack went inside the barn to get insect spray while I filled up the water trough. Suddenly, Steve called out, "Did you see this?" I ran inside the low barn hallway expecting to see a hornet's nest and looked up toward the low-hung ceiling where he pointed. A brown snakeskin about two and a half feet long dangled from a crack in the ceiling. I recoiled as I saw it. In my line of work, I'm used to dealing with dangling participles, not dangling snake skins!

"Holy cow," I said. "Where's the snake?"

"I don't know, but its skin almost smacked me in the face," said my son Jack, who is 6' 5". If it were a snake, it *would* have bitten him.

"Looks like he came through the crack in the ceiling, shed his skin, fell to the floor, and slithered away," said Steve, pointing to the hay-covered floor where I stood. I quickly back stepped out of the barn—right into a pile of manure.

"Think it was a rattler?" asked Jack. "Is it up there now? I think I see something through that crack in the ceiling."

"It's gone," said Steve. "Let's quit worrying about the snake and deal with the hornets." As he walked off to spray the hornets, Jack and I stood studying the dangling snakeskin and the crack above.

The funny thing was that the day before, we had been in and out of the barn and saw, or heard, nothing. I must go in and out of the barn hallway 10 times a day, and I've never thought to look up at the ceiling, and certainly not for a snake. Had we come a few hours earlier I might have met the snake face-to-face, a thought that made my skin crawl. I picked up a stick and removed the snakeskin from the ceiling, then threw it out in the pasture.

"Let's go up and see if we can find the snake," said Jack. I declined. I can't imagine anything worse than walking around on the loft's rickety floor while trying to avoid bumping into a snake.

Back at home, I telephoned Animal Control to see what might be done, and they referred me to a pest control company. The lady who answered the phone was sympathetic and helpful. When I explained the snake was in the barn, she theorized that it might be a rat snake, which made sense. I hadn't seen any mice lately. She said if I could see the snake, the pest control person could come take it away. If not, I could buy snake repellent, an odorous substance.

"I'm told it burns their nostrils," she said.

"Then wouldn't it burn mine?" I asked.

"It smells like mothballs, I'm told," she said. I think when faced with a barn that smells like mothballs, or snakes in the loft, I'd have to choose the latter, especially if the snake eats mice and is not poisonous.

Of course, if we were living in Sicily or Greece back in 400 B.C. I just might be thrilled about the snake hanging around our property. Back then, serpents were a symbol of fertility, and snake-shaped bread was used in a ceremony that was supposed to ensure an abundant harvest. And in some cultures, the snake's shedding its skin and growing a new hide symbolize renewal or immortality.

As for the plain old rat snake in our barn, I'm not sure what it means. I don't really mind if he wants to hang around and keep the rodent population under control. But if the snake has babies, and the barn soon is filled with baby snakes, that's another story. Suppose they all decide to shed their skin at the same time and simultaneously dangle from the ceiling? I just might have to take action. I sure don't want to bump into them and wind up looking like Medusa.

NECESSARY REPAIRS

Georgia, 2013

On a cloudy day a few years ago, I lingered over my hot tea too long and did not arrive at the pasture until the dark clouds had transformed into a downpour. I dashed through the gate and into the barn for cover. Standing on the hay strewn floor, listening to the torrent pound against the tin roof, I felt happy to be out of the rain—until I felt a fat drop of water splash against my cheek.

Looking up, I saw the source of the drip: a hole in the wooden ceiling, the aging boards that make up the floor of our hayloft. I climbed the stairs to the loft to see what was happening. Upstairs, *inside* our barn, it was also raining!

As novel as I found the concept of "indoor rain" I knew the hay bales stored in our loft would soon be ruined if

I didn't take some action. I called my husband, and he quickly came over with some tarps to cover the hay bales.

Within a few weeks we hired a crew to repair the leaky roof. And a whole lot more. The repair turned into a new roof job, and soon green metal was covering the timeworn barn. While working, the roofers found an assortment of rotting beams and suggested those be replaced. And then there were other boards--missing or rotten—essential to keeping the barn standing. Those had to be replaced. And while they were at it, the workmen suggested that an inside, permanent scaffolding be constructed to provide additional support. As so often happens with repair projects, soon the entire barn was getting the works, and it cost us a bundle.

"We could have had a brand new barn," Steve pointed out. "We could have let someone come and take down the barn, pay us for the wood and made enough to pay for a whole new barn."

While a new barn would have been more practical, it would not have held the same memories of our old barn, a place where calves have been birthed, children have tumbled in the loft, and where my grandfather and others tended livestock for about a century.

"It's been there ever since I can remember, and I'm 93," says Mildred Capehart, a Woodstation neighbor. The barn, located on the old Keyes place, came into my family back in the 1940s when my grandfather, Jim Watts, a dairyman, purchased it. Grandpa Watts used it for milking cows, and sometimes for housing cattle and hogs.

During his childhood, Wayne Childers of Ringgold lived near the barn He, his brothers and his friends played in the loft, built tunnels in the hay and played war.

"The object was to try and cave in the opponents' tunnel—with the opponents in it," says Wayne, laughing. His gang also played tag and jumped out of the second-story hay loft for fun, sometimes swinging from a rope. At other times, the boys played rodeo on yearling calves stabled in barn stalls.

"We would hop on the bucking calves and see who could stay on the longest," Wayne recalls.

When I was growing up, the barn and surrounding fields were leased out, so I never played in this barn as a child. Since I moved back here and needed a place to store hay, I got acquainted with the barn and started snooping around for clues of the barn's age.

On a recent rainy day, flashlight in hand, I investigated the interior rooms. The walls are made from both rough-hewn boards and straighter-cut boards. In several places such as the main hallway, aging metal siding serves as a patch. Another board is partly kicked in, a visual reminder of my mare's protest at being penned up.

Some say you can tell a barn's age by its nails. Newer nails are perfect circles while older, hand forged nails are sometimes square, oval, or generally more misshapen. Since most all of the nails on this barn are rusty, it's hard to determine what their original shape was.

In the main hallway, the ceiling hangs low, a result of the barn slowly sinking into the ground. The recently added wooden scaffolding in the main hallway keeps it from further sagging. Doors that lead to two side rooms and to the loft are made up of rough-hewn gray boards that do the job, without being too fancy. The doors stay shut compliments of an old-fashioned wooden latch, or a simple board with a nail driven into the middle that serves as a latch. Other doors are held shut with a nail and chain.

The barn is a hodgepodge of materials. Each variation reflects the many hands that have worked on the barn over the last century to keep it standing.

"I'm glad you saved it," my cousin Waymond Watts tells me. "If we lose our old barns, we lose part of our heritage."

Rains will come and rains will go. Girded by strong, new beams and bearing a new roof, the old barn should weather another decade, providing shelter for livestock, mice, cats and the occasional snoopy human visitor. My old barn will never make the historical register. But like any centenarian, what makes it special is that it has endured.

HUNTING SEASON

"The fascination of shooting as a sport depends almost wholly on whether you are at the right or wrong end of the gun."

—P.G. Wodehouse, The Adventures of Sally

Georgia, 2013

Gunshots pepper the air, announcing to all the world that hunting season is in full swing. While others may pull out their shotguns and rifles, it's time for me to warm up my vocal cords. Let me explain.

I don't hunt, but I want to make sure those who are hunting in the fields all around me know the horses and I are not moving targets. When I walk in the in the field and hear gunshots, I sing. Loudly. Popular tunes, hymns, "God Bless America"—any tune will do. On some days, my notes are wildly off-key, and I make up songs. I'm not sure what the hunters think, but the horses seem to like it.

Even though it's not my best color, I wear red tops and hats during hunting season and pray that hunters don't mistake me for prey.

Even my best efforts to stand out aurally and visually don't always work, like the day last winter when I was out in the field feeding my horses.

I had just caught the horses and tied them up on the round pen rail. I was about to dole out oats. Suddenly, we were all startled by the crack of a rifle shot, and its unmistakable reverberating echo, from just over the fence. The horses spooked, and so did I. Since the fence is covered with thick vegetation, and the field had high grasses, I had no way of knowing if the shooter knew I was there. So, I called out.

"Hey, there's livestock and people over here," I yelled. I talked loudly to the horses and clanged around their feeding buckets. No further gunshots rang out for about five minutes. Then I heard a man's voice from over the fence.

"Ma'am? I'm shooting on my own property, and I'm not aiming the gun toward you," the voice politely informed.

And then, remembering our county laws for those living outside the city limits, I realized the shooter was right.

According to our county sheriff's department, for those living outside the city limits, there are only a few firearms restrictions. The shooter must be at least within 150 feet, or 50 yards from a public street or highway, be on his own property, or if he's on someone else's land, he must have permission from the property owner. He cannot be reckless or endanger the life of another. That's the rule.

Still, bullets that close scare me. Growing up with horses down here in the country, I remember finding at least two of ours shot dead by stray bullets.

Feeling a bit unnerved by my close encounter with my neighboring shooter and wondering what else I might do to protect myself, I called up the Georgia Department of Natural Resources. The gentleman who took my call gave me a few tips. He said I should wear a color called "blaze orange" also known as "hunter orange." "It is the only color that doesn't occur in nature," he said, adding that I would need to wear 500 square inches of it, above the waist. This translates to a hat and vest.

He was very reassuring. He explained that any hunter born after January 1961 must take a hunter education class.

Those older than 51 are grandfathered in and hopefully have enough hunting experience to avoid accidents. Since the inception of mandatory hunter education for the younger set, hunting incidents have gone down. Still, in one recent hunting season, Georgia reported 36 hunting incidents, with 16 of those involving firearms.

Hunters need to be absolutely certain of their target and what is in front of it and beyond it, I learned. For example, if you are in an area with farms and you are shooting a rifle toward an area of trees, or a creek that borders your neighbor's farm, be aware that people or livestock may be on the other side, and within range.

Many of the accidents involve tree stands, not bullets.

Studying a report, I noted four fatalities, three involving tree stand accidents. And oddly enough, most of the accidents were between 6-8 p.m., and the second most happened from 4-6 p.m. The highest number of accidents occurred on Saturdays.

So, if I avoid going to see my horses from 4 to 8 p.m. on Saturdays and stay out of those tree stands, I should be okay. Oh, and I will guess I'll have to put on that unflattering neon orange outfit—although I look a lot better in red. But I wouldn't want any hunters to mistake me for a giant red bird.

And when I hear shooting, I plan to keep singing. Loudly, and probably off-key. After all, one can't be too careful. Who knows? With a little luck, my singing just might scare away the game and the hunters.

HIGH MAINTENANCE FRIEND

"True friendship is seen through the heart, not the eyes."

—Fredrich Nietzsche

Georgia, 2012

If I'd known the trouble ahead, would I ever have become involved with such a high-maintenance friend?

When I first met her, she lured me in with her beauty and her easy manner. Her eyes were friendly and welcoming, her spirits high. Being around her was easy, and I felt like I had known her for years. I am, of course, referring to my dear and costly friend, Fancy, my chocolate-colored mare that came into my life soon after our move to Georgia.

Sold to me as a 10-year-old Arabian–Quarter Horse cross, the vet later checked her teeth and announced, "Let's call her 15, and she's a Morgan." I was so taken with this sweet mare that I had failed to have her checked out before I bought her. In my eagerness to have her, all I thought to ask was "How much will she cost?"

"Plenty, sister," would have been an honest answer. Just like a yacht, a horse is something you pour money into, especially if she has health problems. What I didn't know is that she had, or would soon develop, chronic laminitis (foundering) and an array of associated hoof problems. When she has flare-ups, she must be penned up on a dry lot or in a stable. Either I or a helper must tend to her twice daily, watering, feeding, giving medicines, and cleaning up enough manure to fertilize a bumper crop of tomatoes. Vet bills, medications, supplements, special feed, farriers, and helpers come with a high price tag.

Truth is I am saddled down by a high-maintenance horse. As the months pass by, I continue to learn more than I ever wanted to about the causes of limping. One time, the hoof is bruised and requires several vet visits, antibiotics, and painkillers. Since we have no electricity in the pasture my husband has to haul a portable generator over to the pasture, so an x-ray can be taken. Other times Fancy's limp is caused by abscesses, requiring the farrier or the vet to pay a visit. Another hoof problem calls for foot baths in Epsom salt water every other day. Fancy likes the warm bath and doesn't want to remove her foot when it's time. I can't blame her since it is 36 degrees out. I should know. I carried the thermos of hot water through the cold field. After the bath, her feet are dried off with a clean towel, medicine and pink bandages are applied. What's next, I wonder? Magenta nail polish?

Days of rain lead to white line disease, a fungus or bacterial infection caused by too much moisture. The farrier must cut off large chunks of her front hoof. It hurts. I know this because my mare lowers her body in an effort to kneel on the ground. The vet visits and informs me that medication is required, along with keeping her in a dry stable. Cleaning and medicating her hooves mean that every day I must make my half-ton friend lift her foot, so I can pick out the dirt and squirt on foul-smelling medicine that stains my hands green. Oral antibiotics must be mixed with water and crushed up with molasses or other sweet flavors added to make it palatable.

To tell you the truth, I never knew I'd end up being a horse nurse. As my brother Dean says, "I don't remember all these horse problems when we were kids." Either our horses then were remarkably healthy, or perhaps our dad dealt with it. I remember the vet visiting only one time, when a mare had trouble delivering a colt.

A larger question—a thousand-pound one—is why do I have a special needs horse? And how ridiculous is it that when someone asks, "How are you?" I tell them how Fancy's doing? There are no easy answers.

One winter day when the high was 32 degrees, I felt discouraged as I hunched over her hoof, struggling with the cleaning and medication routine. I rushed to finish before she could put her foot down. To get through this difficult time, I thought of a warm and dry summer day in the pasture when her hoof would be healed, a day when she would glide through the grass like a young filly.

Not realizing I am trying to help her, Fancy resists, much as a human friend might resist help. It's a struggle trying to make her better. Is it worth it?

As my cowboy friend Winston says, she'll never be cured. I know that. Still, as long as there are more good days than bad, I think all the effort is worth it.

High-maintenance friends are a lot of work. Day by day, hour by hour, minute by minute, patience and endurance are required.

The easy days of summer will come again. Warm, dry weather should mean better health for Fancy.

For those of us who have mucked our way through the difficult days, summer is the season to let up a bit, to tend to other things. As for me, with all that manure on hand, I am looking forward to some healthy tomatoes.

THE CHIHUAHUA FAMILY

Georgia, 2008

Soon after we moved to Georgia, we acquired two American Bulldog pups, but not because I wanted them.

"I don't need any dog I can't cradle in my arms," I said, thinking of the Chihuahuas I'd known and loved since I was a child, all six of them. With his sound logic, my son Jack prevailed—we needed a farm dog since we were getting horses. The Georgia-bred Johnson bulldog had been used for herding and even plowing fields.

"Our dogs can help us round up the horses," he said. "You don't want anything smaller than this, Mom. The coyotes might eat them." He had me at "coyotes." I agreed. He promised to care for the new puppies, so I'd be free to care for the horses.

True to his word, Jack walked and trained the dogs. But with two wiggling puppies, two humans were often required to lead them around our backyard. When my husband wasn't available, I reluctantly helped, always pointing out that I hadn't signed on for this.

I kept finding reasons not to like these non-Chihuahuas. Their ears flopped instead of standing up. Their heads were square-shaped, and their snouts blunt. And when they did their business, there was no comparison to my wee dogs.

Two weeks after we brought the pups home, the white one, Bella, wobbled and fell down while I was walking her in our yard. We rushed her to the animal clinic to learn she had Parvo, an often fatal disease. The vet put her in isolation and began treatment.

Alone and frightened in a cage, she fought for her life. When we visited, I was shocked to see once happy Bella slumped over with a hunched back and doleful eyes, IV tubes strapped to her front legs. The vet warned us she probably wouldn't make it. Soon the other bulldog, South, also came down with Parvo and was placed in the cage next to Bella. Every day we made the trip to the clinic in Ringgold to visit. South quickly recovered leaving behind poor Bella, still critically ill. I found myself praying for Bella's recovery. After two long weeks the vet said she was stable enough to come home.

Bella was skin and bones and looked like the emaciated hound on the *Pirates of the Caribbean* ride at Disneyland. I felt sorry for her, so I cooked ground chicken with rice in an effort to fatten her up, just till she got well, of course. After all, she was really Jack's dog, not mine. When no one was looking, I whispered to her and told her when she felt better I'd take her to the pasture. She fixed her gold-brown eyes on me and tilted her head from side to side as though she were trying to understand just what I was saying. I hadn't remembered my Chihuahuas doing that. It made me wonder about what was going on inside that huge head. With her large brain, was she capable of comprehending entire sentences?

Slowly, she recovered and gained weight. Soon, all signs of the Parvo were gone, and she regained her old energy —enough to play and fight. One day, we returned home to find Bella's ears bloody. South and Bella had fought. At the vet's, we learned that females of this breed often fight. The vet recommended we consider getting rid of one of the dogs.

This was a hard decision. We talked about it. Bella was sweet, and South was smart but stubborn. She'd just plop down and refuse to budge. Sweet won out over smart and stubborn. We started looking for a good home for South. On a whim, while talking to an insurance agent on the phone one day, I mentioned our dog dilemma.

"This is weird," said the insurance agent. "Our other dog died, and I've been thinking of getting a new one for my boys." I told her all about South, and within a few days, she brought her two sons out to meet the dog. It was love at first sight. The day we parted with South was a sad one, but we knew it was the right thing to do.

We could focus on Bella, now as big as 10 Chihuahuas. Jack took her to obedience classes and taught her simple commands. Although she often tugged, she could be walked on a leash and would come when called.

One day, when no one else could go with me to the pasture to tend the horses, my husband suggested I take along the bulldog for company. I hesitated. Would she get in my way? Would her training work? When she pleaded with me with those doleful eyes, I gave in. Once we arrived in the spacious pasture, I let her off the leash to run while I searched for the horses.

She saw them before I did and instinctively herded them toward the barn. The gelding, a feisty sorrel, kicked his heels at Bella.

"Watch it, Bella!" I yelled. She pulled away, narrowly avoiding his hooves, and dashed back to me. I leaned over to pat the flat part of her head between those ridiculous floppy ears.

"Good girl," I said. "Watch out for those hooves. We can't have *my* dog getting hurt." She looked at me with her warm brown eyes, cocked her huge head from side to side, and licked my arm with her long pink tongue. Although I hadn't yet realized what I'd just said, Bella had understood every word.

SHADOW, MY FOOT!

"Do you ever have déjà vu?"

–Rita, a character in the movie, Groundhog Day

Georgia, 2011

In Punxsutawney, Pennsylvania, a groundhog named Phil may spend winter days coming out to look for his shadow, or preening for news cameras that come out to capture a shot of him exiting his burrow. Down here in North Georgia, our groundhogs seem to be too busy causing trouble to worry about Groundhog Day.

One winter morning when Steve and I go to the pasture to water the horses, we turn on the faucet and find nothing coming out of the hose up by the troughs. One of the garden hoses that carries water some 200 feet is bitten in two.

"Could it be coyotes?" I ask.

"See those tiny teeth marks?" asks Steve. "Had to be something smaller, like a groundhog." So, we leave the pasture, pop in the car, and head out to buy a new $39 length of hose. Two weeks later, the "groundhog" strikes again, leaving the hose chewed right in half. Twice in three weeks. The situation feels like déjà vu. Seeing the second gnawed-apart hose, Steve and I head to the hardware up in Ringgold. Again.

"We need a garden hose, and a trap," he says as we walk through the aisles. A humane trap runs around $50, and the new 100-foot hose another $39. So far, the groundhog is into us for about $130.

Since I've never trapped a groundhog before, I study the directions and learn they like to eat apples, but also okra leaves, tomatoes, and carrots. Rubber garden hoses are not mentioned. The directions suggest setting up the trap by the animal's den.

"Should be easy," I say.

"What?"

"Finding the den. Let's just look for a big-screen TV." Steve doesn't laugh. So much for my pasture humor. Instead, he theorizes the hole is somewhere near the chewed-up hose.

I think it's down by the creek. We walk around for half an hour looking and find not a single hole. Why is it so easy to stumble into holes when I'm riding my horse but almost impossible when I am on foot looking for a den where I can set a trap? One of those inconvenient truths.

Steve finally announces we should just set the trap at the scene of the crime—err, the gnawed apart hose. He carefully loads apple and carrot pieces into the back of the trap and places the latch in place. Now it's a waiting game until Mr. Groundhog is tempted by the fruit.

Of course, catching him will lead to the next question: how will we get rid of him? I am thinking of driving him up to the top of Taylor's Ridge and letting him out in the woods. Although the critter would have no hoses up there to feast upon, the view of the Valley is spectacular. Maybe he could even try chucking some wood for a change.

"What if he finds his way back to our pasture and eats another hose in half?" asks Steve. He prefers another method, one that involves a pistol and bullets.

What would we do with the body? Steve thinks the buzzards will take care of it, but I'm not sure. I call and ask my brother, Dean, how he would dispose of the body if, of course, we catch it.

"I hear the funeral home is having a special on groundhog caskets," he replies. "You can get a package deal for $100. I'll even drive down for the memorial service."

I ask around to find out what other folks think. My farrier thinks rats are chewing up the hoses.

"They need to file down their teeth, or they'd grow too long," he says. Of course, groundhogs are simply large rodents, cuter than their rat cousins. My brother speculates it's probably rabbits, recalling a TV show where a man kept finding something wreaking havoc in his garden. Thinking it must be a mischievous neighbor, the man bought a surveillance camera and placed it in the garden, only to find it was a pesky rabbit. I think I can do without a pricey surveillance camera, but I ponder alternatives—like getting a hose the rat-rabbit-groundhog can't sink its teeth into—one coated with a galvanized steel shell.

Remarkably, I find one listed on the internet for about $339, the length we need, a hundred feet. Times two. At this cost, I might as well rent a ditch witch and lay in PVC pipe.

A week, then two, pass without any creatures going for the bait in our humane trap. The thermometer dips down to the teens. Perhaps the critters don't care about the pitiful, shriveled, and frozen fruit lying in the back of the cage. Or maybe when it's this cold, the rat-rabbit-groundhog is too busy shivering to worry about filing down its teeth.

When the weather warms up, a very long-toothed groundhog may come out of his burrow for another taste of our new $39 hose. One thing's for sure. If that groundhog shows up in our pasture when my husband's around, he'd better be wearing a Kevlar vest. The dirty rat.

A NEIGHBORLY VISIT

"Always ready to do everything in his power

for his friends and neighbors."

—From the obituary of A. G. Dunn, "Catoosa County

Record," March 26, 1908

Georgia, 2011

While researching a story for my magazine column I learned of the Dunn sisters, Evelyn and Eloise, longtime Woodstation residents and the great-granddaughters of a Catoosa County pioneer, A. G. Dunn.

"You have to meet them," said the gentleman I was interviewing. "They have an old envelope bearing a Woodstation postmark." Since I hadn't even realized Woodstation ever had a post office, I was determined to pay the Dunn sisters a visit and see the envelope.

On a sunny summer morning, I pulled in past a row of lush lavender crepe myrtles that lined their driveway and parked my car. Before I could even reach the front door, Evelyn and Eloise rushed out onto the sidewalk to warmly greet me. They invited me into their living room to see the letter, but I found greater treasure in hearing their stories of growing up in Woodstation in the 1930s and 1940s.

The daughters of the late Gladys and Judson Dunn, the sisters showed me two dolls they received when they were three and six. The dolls arrived wearing only diapers, one in blue and one in pink. That would be their most memorable Christmas gift for some time. Their father died when they were six and nine, and from then on, Christmas gifts consisted of an apple or an orange, which they felt lucky to receive. Along with their mother, the two sisters moved in with their grandparents, Mattie and Jim Dunn, at their home near Hullender and West Nickajack Roads.

The sisters started school at the old Woodstation School located next to the present Woodstation Church. During their school years, two of their teachers were relatives, Miss Addie Dunn, a second cousin, and Mrs. Clara Dunn, their aunt by marriage, who was described as a good teacher but strict, except when it came to dogs. Eloise's pet spitz would sometimes follow her to school, but Mrs. Dunn would let the dog stay inside the classroom. The dog sat patiently on the floor next to Eloise most of the time.

"When I went up to the blackboard to write, he'd follow me up to the front," she said.

Money was scarce for their widowed mother. The girls earned a little money picking and chopping cotton. Eloise recalls the time they were helping a sharecropper family chop cotton and were asked to help catch a possum.

"They put the possum up in a pen and fed it for a month, then ate it," said Eloise. "They wanted me to try it, but I said no, thank you. It looked like fried chicken."

To earn extra money, the girls also hiked up the dirt road leading to the top of Taylor's Ridge and picked huckleberries to sell. When not working trying to earn a little money, they kept busy at their grandma's home with chores.

"Once a week, Grandma would fill up a huge wash pot with water from the spring," said Evelyn. "She'd build a fire under it, add some lye soap or octagon, put the clothes in, and use a punch stick to push the clothes into the water. We had to help her wash, iron, and make our own starch from flour."

Canning was done differently back then, according to Evelyn, before modern stoves were in use.

"My mother canned in the wash tub," she said. "She set it on top of bricks and built a fire underneath."

Discussing life back in the 30s and 40s and now, Eloise said life was much harder back then than it is now. "I don't know what today's people would do if they lived back then," said Eloise. "They don't seem to work like people did when we were growing up."

Despite all the hard work, the girls found time to have a little fun. On the way to school, about a mile or two walk, the girls liked to cut through neighboring farms. On hot days, they stopped at the local swimming hole located on the Little Chickamauga Creek that ran through the old Keyes' farm off Nickajack Road. Wading in the creek one day, Evelyn decided to try out the rope swing suspended from a tree.

"I grabbed the rope, swung out, and dropped into the creek and liked to have drowned," she said.

On Sunday mornings, the sisters climbed into their aunt and uncle's wagon, pulled by mules, and drove across Taylor's Ridge on the steep dirt road, which is now East Nickajack. After attending Hickory Grove Baptist Church, they would journey to their uncle's sister's place for a family dinner.

"There was always lots of good food and plenty of children to play with," said Eloise. "They had a lot of kids."

Back in Woodstation at home, the sisters looked forward to the weekly arrival of Willie Childers' rolling store.

"It was a closed-in truck filled with everything we didn't have on the farm," says Eloise. "Sugar, coffee, candy, and such. And you could pay him in chickens, and in the back of the truck, he had a chicken coop where he put the chickens."

As the girls grew older, they joined friends and went roller skating down at Lake Howard in Walker County, to the movie theater in Fort Oglethorpe, and to drive-in movies near Rossville. Along with other girls in the community, some of them also sisters, Evelyn and Eloise started a girls' softball team that played in the field by the Woodstation School. Their team competed against teams at Mt. Pisgah, Boynton, Ringgold, and at Warner Park in Chattanooga through the late 40s.

Since Woodstation was far from Ringgold, and a small, close-knit community, everyone knew each other, and neighbors were quick to help one another if needed. In the

1930s and early '40s, of those living on the west side of Little Chickamauga Creek, only two families had cars.

"When you needed a ride into town, you had to ask a neighbor," said Eloise." You knew everybody in the community, but it's not that way now." After she got her first car, a used '41 Chevy, Eloise was the one offering rides.

"A neighbor came over and asked if I could drive him and his wife into Ringgold to the doctor's," said Eloise. "His headlights were broken, and she was about to have a baby." She and Evelyn climbed into the front of the car while the couple got in the back. Evelyn handed some clean sheets back to the husband to place over the car seat. Eloise sped north on the Old Alabama Highway, then a gravel road. When she arrived in Ringgold, she learned the woman had delivered the baby en route near the Yates farm.

"I overheard the husband telling Dr. Stephenson, 'We had a race with the stork, and we lost,'" she said. "I was glad the baby was okay, but I couldn't help thinking of my car seat, probably ruined." Fortunately, the new father offered to pay to have the seat cleaned.

After graduating from Ringgold High, the two sisters moved closer to their jobs in the textile industry but visited their Woodstation family on weekends. Evelyn worked at the

Hosiery Mill and the Chickamauga Bleachery but spent the majority of her working years at Candlewick Yarns in Ringgold. Eloise spent most of her career at Dixie Yarns in Chattanooga and joined the company softball team. Both girls dated but never married.

"A gang of us girls were always going somewhere and having fun playing softball, skating, or going to the movies," said Eloise. "It seemed like we had more fun being with our gang than we did dating."

In the 1970s, after their mother passed on, the sisters came back to Woodstation to care for their stepfather. They now live in a home on a plot of land next to where the family home once stood.

When I first met them, they no longer held down outside jobs, but "retired" does not describe their active lives. Evelyn embroiders and works on quilt tops, while Eloise works on counted cross-stitch and quilts. They attend church regularly and enjoy spending time with cousins. In summertime, they tend their own garden and help their neighbors with shucking and removing silks from corn grown in their garden. The neighbors share their harvest with Evelyn and Eloise. Working as a team, during one hot July week, the sisters and their neighbors canned 21 quarts of beans.

And what about that letter with the Woodstation postmark that prompted my visit? Eloise showed me several envelopes bearing a Woodstation postmark and two-cent stamps. She told me the family connection to the post office: their grandfather's first wife, Caroline Wilbanks Dunn, was the postmistress at Woodstation post office, located on the Old Alabama Highway near the former Trundle's Store building.

As I prepared to leave, Evelyn asked me if I would like something from their garden. Eloise ran to the kitchen for a minute and returned with a huge bag of yellow squash, which I gratefully received.

Even though many years have passed since they grew up in the Woodstation community, the Dunn sisters are eager to share their bounty, continuing the local tradition of being good neighbors learned so well in their childhood.

THE DUNN SISTERS—REVISITED

Georgia, 2019

In the eight years after I met them, I often saw Eloise out on her riding lawnmower on the hottest of days wearing her wide-brimmed hat. Keeping their lawn mowed was one of her priorities. I stopped by to see them and always welcomed their gifts of okra, garlic, or tomatoes which they had in abundance. If I had my grandchildren with me, I'd take them in to visit the sisters who had known my Grandfather Watts when they were little. Eloise would pull out an animated dancing chicken and watch the children laugh as the chicken belted out its tune and flapped its fluffy arms. Eloise and Evelyn laughed too!

One afternoon, my phone rang. A friend called to tell me the sad news. Eloise, the taller sister, had died. One day, as was her ever-industrious fashion, she cleaned out her refrigerator and then walked outdoors to throw away the trash. When she hadn't come back inside for a time, sister Evelyn went out and found her on the ground, unresponsive. Everyone who knew the sisters was heavy-hearted, but none so much as Evelyn.

For a few more years, Evelyn carried on alone. I stopped by several times to visit, but our visits were more formal and shorter. Sister-less for the first time in her life, she was like one-half of a comedy routine. Several years later, Evelyn also died. I was sad to hear not only of her passing but of the death of this link to the past; however, the sisters left behind their houseful of treasures.

Soon, the "For Sale" sign went up in their yard. An estate sale sign followed. I knew I had to go.

By the time I arrived at the sale, many of the dolls and figurines were gone. As I wandered through rooms of all their belongings, I spotted a painting that summed up an earlier time, a farmer in overalls plowing a field using a mule. An old barn stood in the distance. This reminded me of the sisters' young lives on the farm. As I moved closer to retrieve the farm picture, I spotted a fluffy pastel chicken on the dresser. The dancing chicken! I smiled when I saw it, remembering the sisters' playful side. The children would love it.

Back at home, I put the chicken in with the children's stuffed animals and placed the farmer plowing painting into a corner of my office. I waited to let the grandchildren discover the chicken amongst the stuffed bears, monkeys, dogs, and unicorns.

When the pandemic hit, we kept the grandchildren at home. The days were long and often trying as we stayed away from people who might have the virus. My grandson turned to the toy basket and sorted through, pulled out the colorful pastel chicken. He placed it on the hardwood floor and hit the "on" switch. The "Chicken Dance" music filled the room, and he danced in circles, motioning his younger sister to join him.

Watching the children running and circling the dancing chicken, giggling nonstop, I remembered the two sisters. I could see their contagious smiles and hear their laughter. Through a simple, silly toy, the Dunn sisters' playful spirit lived on.

MESSAGES ON WHEELS

Georgia, 2012

Driving along the country roads every day, I receive an unexpected gift. You know, the little hand gesture that means, "hello," "goodbye," or in my neck of the woods, "howdy neighbor" even if you aren't acquainted with the person waving at you.

When I first moved here, I was pleasantly surprised by complete strangers greeting me. I had forgotten how friendly people can be. In California, strangers usually don't wave except on a crowded freeway when another driver might wave to indicate permission to pull into his lane. Or not. Then the agitated driver might make another hand gesture, one using a single digit.

Why do people down here wave to complete strangers? I asked a professor of communication.

"The wave is a form of non-verbal communication, meaning any message that transcends or goes beyond words," she said. "The wave is a sign that friendliness is more common and expected in the rural South," she said. "Why? People are friendlier in the South, probably because it was an agrarian culture, and community was seen as more necessary for survival. Also, in general, the closer cultures are to the Equator, and the warmer the weather, the more relaxed the culture is. Mediterranean culture is far more relaxed than British or Northern European, for example."

In some cultures, a waving cat conveys a message of good luck. A common Japanese sculpture, Maneki Neko, the "Beckoning Cat" or "Lucky Cat," is also popular with the Chinese. The ceramic sculpture depicts a cat waving with one paw or another. A left-pawed wave is said to attract money, while a wave with the right paw is said to protect money. I recently spotted one of these in a Ringgold restaurant when I went there for take-out, but I was too hungry to notice which paw the cat was waving.

I could use one of those lucky cats. I would want the type with both paws waving, one paw to bring in the money and the other one to help me keep it. And as long as I'm wishing, I think I would like a dog waving both its front paws. A white bulldog would be nice. But I digress …

For now, I'll stick to humans waving. Since moving to Georgia, on the back roads, I've received hundreds of waves and observed several types.

First, there's the one-fingered wave, using the index finger. The driver of a passing vehicle will raise his index finger while gripping the steering wheel. This wave says, "I want to acknowledge you, but I am not going to commit entirely to saying howdy in case you don't wave back." Or it could be that the driver needs to keep a good grip on the wheel since his other hand is wrapped around a cup of hot coffee or a cell phone.

Another version of this wave is four-fingers lifted in greeting, with the thumb remaining hooked under the steering wheel. While I like this more committed version of saying howdy, I admit I worry when the driver is in a truck or a minivan, and we're passing each other on a narrow stretch of road. I can only hope the driver has a strong thumb.

My favorite is the full-out wave where the driver lifts his hand off the steering wheel, showing all four fingers, thumb, and full palm. This driver knows the importance of a whole-hearted wave, and most likely has the steering wheel under control with his other hand, or I sure hope so. I worry he may lose control of his car while waving at me, and I'd hate that. Of course, the person giving a full-out wave is probably a happy-go-lucky sort and doesn't worry about running off the road.

Another wave, often observed in warmer weather, is the hanging-the-hand-out-of-the-window wave. This person is a friendly type who loves the feel of the cool wind on her palm. Or perhaps she is drying off her hands after spilling that cup of sweet tea all over the emergency brake. Either way, the hanging-the-hand-out-of-the-window wave always makes my day.

In the winter, on overcast days when my mood matches the gloomy skies, a single wave makes me feel everything is going to be alright. When I see that wave, I think, hey, we are all living under the same gray, sometimes black, clouds, yet this passing driver, this fellow traveler, has made the effort to greet me. We are all Southerners, and we stick together.

My reaction to a simple gesture was strongest right after the tornado, when any type of wave could cause me to tear up. To me, a wave said, "We are survivors, we're still here, we'll be alright."

Of course, some folks don't wave. No problem. I figure they are otherwise preoccupied. I don't take it personally. But you know what? When I can pry my hand off my iced tea in time, I give them a big wave anyway. After all, we are fellow travelers on the road. The world is a friendlier place for those blessed by a greeting that requires nothing but a simple lift of the hand.

BARN SWALLOWS

Georgia, 2015

In Southern California, the annual return of the Mission San Juan Capistrano swallows is a rite of spring. On, and sometimes before March 19, St. Joseph's Day, the swallows' arrival at the mission attracts flocks of tourists. During the 1970s, I was one of those who waited every spring to see the swallows return to this charming mission town.

The little birds that flew in and perched atop the 200-year-old mission walls didn't look like the swallows I'd seen growing up in the South. The California swallows were cliff swallows, I discovered. Still, their faithful return held a mystical appeal.

On a spring day down at the farm, I looked up from horse chores to see a swallow fly by as he headed for our run-in shed where my mare Fancy lives with our barn cat, Amie.

Soon, another swallow swooped past. The pair cruised low as they flew through the shed and back out again. Seeing their forked tails, I knew at once that they were barn swallows.

Stuffing hay into the net feeding bag, I glanced up at the roof to see a nest attached to a high beam near the entrance. A swallow's nest! The pair flew through again, checking me out.

"I bet we're going to have some baby swallows soon," I told Amie. Her tail twitched as she gazed up at the nest.

For the next few weeks, I noticed the swallows swooping in and out of the barn and sometimes sitting on the nest. I couldn't see any eggs, but I knew they were there. The swallows sometimes perched on a beam at the other end of the shed, observing me.

"I'm not going to hurt your babies," I reassured the pair. Because they eat flies and hornets, the swallows are welcomed at my run-in. Since their arrival, I had noticed fewer insects.

One morning, I arrived at the run-in to find the swallows dive bombing the cat. As I tried to pass by the fray, I felt the soft flutter of wings against my arm. I followed Amie inside. She curled up beside a cluster of hay strewn on the floor, batting her paw. Hiding inside the hay cluster was a tiny, dark bird. A baby swallow. I felt sick to my stomach. I pulled Amie away and scooped up the hay and baby bird, careful not to touch it. Its breath was shallow, but it was alive. Looking around the run-in, I decided to place the barely alive bird at the highest point where I hoped the cat couldn't reach —the top of an upturned feeding bucket attached to a metal gate high off the ground. I hoped that the cat couldn't climb up the metal bars, that somehow the parents would rescue their fledgling. I turned around to scold Amie.

"Bad cat!" I said. I waved my arms to shoo her away. She sidled up against my legs. I walked away, ignoring her. Even though I know it's her nature to hunt, I was angry. In fact, had she knocked a mouse silly, I would have praised her. Why do we humans like one species better than another? It makes no sense.

Walking back through the pasture, I pondered what happened. Despite the swallow parents' vigilance, their swooping and circling the nest for days, their baby ended up on the ground batted around like catnip. These birds are not unlike human helicopter parents who hover over their children, doing their best to protect their young, yet not always in control of what happens once the children go out on their own.

"They were excellent parents," I said to Bella, my American bulldog, who tagged along by my side. "I hope they rescue that baby." She stared at me with her big brown eyes as though she understood.

The next morning, I rushed to the pasture, hopeful I'd see the fledgling gone from the high place I'd left it. But as I entered the shed, I glanced down and saw a dark, still, lifeless form lying in the barn dust. The cat had won the battle.

A week or so later, I entered the shed. A single white feather floated down from the rafters, then another. A barn swallow circled around, checking me out. She flew up to a new nest—a home attached to the highest beam in the shed, well out of the cat's reach. She settled in carefully, on her new eggs, I assumed. A second chance.

I never saw any fledglings, and one day in July, I realized I hadn't seen the swallow parents either. Where did they go? Did they take the kids away? Had they migrated early to Florida or even Central America? Could they in fact be sipping Margaritas on a beach somewhere? A happy ending for them, I hoped.

But not for me. In the run-in one morning, reaching for a curry comb to groom the horses, I instead found a swarm of hornets. Before I could pull my hand away, I felt a sharp burn on my right wrist. Stung!

Running cool water over my forearm, I saw three red marks and realized the obvious. The swallows were gone, the hornets were back, and my wrist was starting to swell. Their departure hurt!

I hope the swallow family enjoys their vacation. Come spring, I'll be waiting for their return just as I waited for the swallows back in California so many years ago.

Some things never change.

DREAMING OF A WHITE CHRISTMAS

Georgia, 2012

Last Christmas morning, about the time I turned on the stove to heat up the tea kettle, the snow started falling. For the next several hours white flakes came down, and soon five inches of snow covered the ground. I didn't have to dream about it—a white Christmas had appeared in my own backyard.

As lovely as the view was from my window, the snow meant more work out in the pasture where our horses live. Faucets often freeze, and water would have to be ferried back. If the water is frozen, or too cold, our horses won't drink. To encourage drinking in freezing weather, we would have to carry hot water in plastic jugs to the horses.

"Let's get going before it gets worse," I said to Steve, who seemed content to linger over his hot tea. I gathered empty yellow plastic containers—five gallons each—and started filling them up with hot water. After filling four, I changed into long johns, pants, T-shirt, sweatshirt, jacket, scarf, hat, gloves, and boots, my usual costume for winter weather. I had on so many layers I could hardly move.

"The Stay Puff Marshmallow man returns," I said, waddling out to our four-wheel drive wagon, our vehicle of choice when traction is dicey. Steve laughed. He loaded the heavy jugs into the cargo area while Bella scrambled into the back seat, panting in anticipation. To her, a trip to the pasture is like going to Disneyland.

We drove slowly through our neighborhood, passing snowball fighters and snowman builders alike, all grabbing up handfuls of the white stuff. Arriving at the barn, I poured generous portions of feed into buckets while Steve grabbed several hay flakes to load into our wagon.

Proceeding through the snow, deeper in the pasture than it was on the road, we were able to drive back to where the horses waited, their ears perked up, their nostrils blowing fog.

Steve unloaded the water jugs. At the trough, he broke a layer of ice into pieces and cast it aside, then poured in the water, now warm. Fancy, my mare, observed the rising steam.

"Teatime," said Steve in a British accent. Fancy dipped her nose into the water, took a long sip, seeming to enjoy the warm liquid.

"Crumpets," said Steve. He extended a bucket of feed. Sunny rushed over and attacked the "crumpets." After watering, feeding, and petting the horses, we left, happy to have had another pasture visit.

With the January snows, we were not so fortunate. The snow was deeper. While parked alongside the barn, our wagon was hit by a mini avalanche of snow that slid off the barn roof. When we attempted to pull away, the tires spun. We were stuck. Thankfully, our son, Jack, was with us to help Steve lug the water back on foot. I carried feed and hay. We humans had become the beasts of burden, while the horses stood waiting to be served their "tea and crumpets."

After caring for the horses, we returned to our wagon and shoveled. Two hours later, we finally succeeded in freeing the car and headed home for own tea.

For the next day's visit to the pasture, Steve came up with a new transportation mode to carry the warm water back.

"Bella can earn her keep," he said. He rolled a tarpaulin onto the ground, put a harness on our dog, and attached a rope from the harness to the tarp, where he had placed the four jugs of water. Side-by-side, man and dog worked as a team pulling the tarp through the snow. Bella seemed to know what to do, but I was not surprised. Her breed, American Bulldog, was bred to plow fields.

As I watched them pull, I couldn't help laughing.

"What?" asked Steve.

"Instead of us riding in a one-horse open sleigh, you and Bella are pulling a sled to the horses," I said.

"It's a tarp," said Steve. "Wanna try?" I did not.

With winter's arrival, I have been pondering the notion of another white Christmas. I telephoned a few long-time residents to get their thoughts.

Barbara Watts, my aunt, said she remembered one snowy Christmas in the 1930s when she lived just over Taylor's Ridge in the Houston Valley area. Her daddy wanted to get her a doll but couldn't get to town because of the snow.

"He saddled up his horse and rode to the highway, then found a ride into town with someone who had a car," she said. "I got that doll."

Mildred Capehart, who lived in the Woodstation area her entire life, said there were more snows back then.

"I don't remember that many white Christmases, though." She recalled riding in a sleigh when she was a girl in the 1920s.

"The horse would be hooked to the singletree and would pull the sleigh. We also would go a lot in the wagon."

Thinking Mrs. Capehart might share her frigid weather wisdom, I asked her how folks watered livestock back then when their faucets froze up.

"Freezing faucets?" she asked. "Why we didn't have running water when I was growing up!"

SIGNPOSTS IN TORNADO LAND

Georgia, 2011

A few nights after a tornado ripped through Ringgold, Georgia, I drove down the Old Alabama Highway, one of the main roads leading into town. Usually this thoroughfare, exit 348 off the I-75, is lit with bright signs advertising food, shelter, and gas. This night it was dark, yet from the car lights of the freeway I could see the pale outline of topsy-turvy stick buildings and bare poles where the tall beacons of modern American civilization used to glow.

With my car windows down, evening smells drifted through. Not the familiar aroma of French fries, but the scent of fresh wood and upturned earth, smells usually associated with new construction but now with destruction. In these first days of May, parts of the city look like a ghost town, a place where some have lost their lives or been left homeless.

Much of the area surrounding Ringgold is rural, a place of green velvet fields, gentle ridges, and lazy streams dotted with cows and horses. I spent much of my childhood on our family farm in the south end of Catoosa County, in a valley alongside Taylor's Ridge, and returned many years later seeking a return to a gentle life with animals and nature. Tornadoes were not in the plan.

When we first arrived, I complained about the gigantic signs that might give visitors the wrong impression of our town when they got off the freeway onto the main thoroughfare leading into town. Yet I realized the signs could be what lured thirsty and hungry drivers off the freeway and into our town in the first place. I always hoped the curious might drive a little farther to discover our history, the railroad depot, stores brimming with antiques, or the Chowtime, a 1960s diner and a local hangout.

After living eight miles out in the country for a couple of years, I began to see the signposts that lined the thoroughfare differently. They came to represent civilization, a place where I could find hot food, a smile, and sometimes a minute of friendly conversation, a welcome change from the solitude of the country life.

On my first night seeing the tornado destruction up close, what I noticed most was the absence of light. No bright signs to light up the sky—only empty metal frames atop tall signposts. Electricity had not been restored in this area where 175 mph winds brought new meaning to the words "drive through." At Hardee's, an 80-foot sign had toppled into, and embedded itself, in the roof. It jutted out from the rooftop reminding me of the barrel of a Civil War cannon.

As I left the ghost town behind and headed back to the country, I kept thinking of that fallen pole atop Hardee's, poised like a cannon about to be fired, a signpost that seemed to convey another message. Ringgold was ready for the fight to rebuild itself.

THE GEORGIA FIVE

Georgia, 2010

Right before I left for my new home in Georgia, my Beverly Hills hairdresser, a stylishly slim fellow, said, "Now don't you get fat when you move down South."

"Why would you say that?" I asked.

"Honey, I lived in Arkansas, I know what I'm talking about." I laughed. "I don't think so," I said. As if living in Arkansas could be compared to living in Georgia! Isn't Arkansas almost the Midwest?

But now, after living here for several years, indulging in the local specialties, I began to understand what my hairdresser was talking about. With an abundance of vegetables (fried okra and fried green tomatoes, cheesy squash casserole, hammy green beans, and turnip greens cooked with fatback) and hot pulled shredded pork barbecue with a touch of sauce and chilled coleslaw, it's hard not to over-indulge. And biscuits, and gravy. Chicken-fried steak, and gravy. Grits and gravy. And just about anything else and gravy.

Gravy is the glue that holds the South together, I've about decided. A belly full of warm gravy fortifies and soothes the nerves in the midst of a harried day. Gravy is the South's version of meditation. And properly prepared, gravy makes you think of slower times when the cook stirred the gravy till it was just right. You can't rush your gravy.

And biscuits? Once, while eating breakfast out one morning, I overheard two ladies at the next table in an intense biscuit discussion. What was best? Drop biscuits, or rolled biscuits? Regular or buttermilk? And what about—heaven forbid—canned biscuits? One of the ladies admitted to having cooked and served canned biscuits to guests.

"They were pretty good," she said. The other woman (rather haughtily, it seemed) replied, "Oh really? I've never eaten canned." A weighty silence followed.

After a big meal of biscuits and gravy, of heavily breaded fried this, and that, there's no point in stopping, or at least until the peach cobbler or red velvet cake has been tasted. And while sharing a dessert with a loved one, the conversation seems to always turn to the next meal, be it church potluck, cookie exchange, or lunch at a country restaurant. Sometimes, when I'm homesick for California, I might visit one of the local Mexican places and snack on crispy corn chips and salsa while eating a couple of enchiladas drowning in cheese. The Georgia version of Mexican food seems to be topping everything with a pound of gooey, melted cheese.

As for portion control, none is allowed down here. The plates are filled entirely, with portions large enough to feed a big and tall man, or tempting enough to feed a regular-sized woman with a big appetite. Besides, who wants to bother lugging half the meal home in those Styrofoam "to go" containers, anyway? Might as well join the clean plate club … using that final biscuit to clean up the last drop of gravy.

After living here for a while, I have now gained a new perspective about "getting fat," as my hairdresser termed it. I call this phenomenon "The Georgia Five," referring not to a gang of criminals but rather to that extra poundage that has crept up under my elastic waist pants while I indulged in the delicious foods of my native South. At this rate, pigs will fly before I ever slim down to a 17-inch, Scarlett O'Hara waist.

And speaking of flying pigs, let's hope when those porkers finally land, it'll be right into a nearby smoky barbecue pit.

I have spoken with other recent arrivals and found the phenomenon to be rather … widespread. Some say I'm wrong, that I should call it "The Georgia Eight" and some suggest "The Georgia Ten." (Hey, I didn't force them to eat that extra slice of coconut cream pie!) None of us seems too worried about our new perspective, and I'm sure after we've settled in, we'll cut back a bit. The food will become less and less of a novelty and more routine. We'll no doubt cut back on gravy, biscuits, and fried this and that, and start eating more salads. We'll tell them to hold the gravy, grill the chicken, and leave off that crispy, crunchy golden coating that melts in our mouths. Yes, we will. You can bet your flying pig on it!

CUTTING LOOSE

"All good things are wild and free." —Henry David Thoreau

Georgia, 2009

On July 14, 2009, while folks over in France were celebrating Bastille Day, their Independence Day, I was driving down to the barn to meet the farrier before it got too hot to venture out. Down in Woodstation, Georgia it was a typical early summer morning, or so I thought.

When I arrived at the barn, the horses stood waiting at the gate as though they were expecting me. I pulled into the driveway, hopped out, and unlatched the gate, so I could pull in beside the barn. They wouldn't budge from their position by the gate, and I waved my arms to shoo them to the side. To my surprise, they disregarded me, walked right past me through the open gate, and headed for the tall, dark green grass by the side of the road. Worried that a car could soon pass and startle them, I tried to lure them back with a bag of apples pulled from my belt pack. They ignored me, preferring to graze instead. I tried to remain calm.

"Sunny, here's your treat," I said, placing an apple in my mouth and making exaggerated chewing sounds. Sunny glanced up with a look that said, "Who cares?" He turned away, clip clopped onto the asphalt with the mare right trailing behind. Then it hit me—we had a situation. The horses were now trotting down West Nickajack Road headed in the direction of the Old Alabama Highway. They could be hit by a car at any moment! I went into high gear, determined to catch them before any cars drove by. I called my sister on the cell phone and told her to come quickly with a halter, rope, and a bucket of feed.

Instead of heading for greener pastures, Sunny trotted over to the pair of pretty mares next door. I jogged along behind. Head and tail held high, he moved off the road and pranced across a neighbor's lawn. Sunny craned his neck over the barbed wire fence to touch noses with the mares while I crept up near his side, knowing this was my chance to catch him. In my palm, I held out an apple slice. He sniffed and took a bite. I snapped off my belt pack and fashioned a noose around his neck. Not wanting him to escape again, I looped my finger between the belt and his face and held on tightly. We started toward the barn with the mare following.

Suddenly, Sunny threw up his head and jerked away, almost yanking off my middle finger, which was tangled in the makeshift halter. I watched as he trotted away. Surprisingly, the mare didn't follow him but walked back toward the barn. I turned and saw my sister Judy approaching with a bucket of feed. We easily caught the mare and haltered her.

"You take her back, I'll go after him," I said. Running along behind Sunny, I saw he was now headed for a hay field some distance away. An approaching jeep slowed down.

"Want some help?" asked the driver. It was a neighbor, Shannon, whom I've known since childhood.

"Yes!" I said. He motioned me to get in. I jumped in, and he turned the jeep around and drove over to the field where my gelding was checking out some round bales of hay.

"I'll stop the cars while you try to catch him," he said. I nodded and climbed out of the jeep with the feed bucket. Sunny took a step toward those apples, snorted, and pulled away, ready not for a snack but for a real adventure. He trotted away and headed back down the road leading to our farm. I jumped back into Shannon's jeep, and we followed.

Predictably, Sunny once again stopped by to flirt with the two shapely mares. With feed bucket in my hand, I stood on the side of the yard trying to figure out what to do next while trying to block out the pain from my swollen, throbbing middle finger. I looked up to see an old red Chevy truck driving down the road. The answer to my prayers, my farrier. He got out of his truck and pulled out a rope. I handed him the feed bucket. With rope and feed in hand, he approached and easily captured the gelding.

After I'd thanked everyone and gotten the horses back to the barn for their hoof trims, I realized how much my finger hurt. Later that day, I would find out I had a compound fracture. Sunny? He seemed nonchalant about his adventurous morning. After all, he'd had a nice visit with the two beauties in the next pasture over and enjoyed his impromptu tour of Woodstation.

As I left our barn and headed to the doctor to get my finger x-rayed, I passed the yellow caution sign near our barn that has a drawing of a horse and rider. I laughed, thinking a more appropriate drawing might be a picture of fleeing horses being chased by people.

Sometimes an ordinary day can turn out to be anything but. I'm thankful for having a sister and a neighbor both willing to drop what they were doing to help me catch the horses, for a farrier with a rope in his truck and a knack for getting horses to mind. As for the horses escaping that morning, I finally figured out why. Like the French, they were simply celebrating their freedom.

ROYAL POO-PAH

Caveat emptor (Latin for "let the buyer beware")

Georgia, 2011

You may have been tempted by the magazine ad showing a towering tree with lavender blossoms. A tree that produces a rich fragrance and shoots up to 12 feet in one growing season. A tree with large heart-shaped leaves that pull pollution out of the air. A tree that was named after Russian royalty. Yes, joy can be yours for a mere $12.98, plus shipping and handling.

Drawn in by the picture of the huge tree awash in my favorite color, I sent off a check and started watching the mailbox. According to the mail-order nursery, the trees, which I nicknamed "The Royal Poo-Pahs," were supposed to ship at "the appropriate arrival time in my region," whatever that meant. Winter turned to spring, and still I waited, wondering if I had been rooked. One day, when I had almost forgotten about my trees, a tiny box marked "live plants" arrived. Inside was a pair of two-inch-tall green plants. I showed my husband the measly little things.

"Surely there's been a mistake. These look like house plants," I said.

"That'll teach you to order out of a magazine."

"We'll see," I said, and retreated to the garage to get some pots and dirt. After transplanting the seedlings, I gently tamped down the dark soil to make them cozy in their new home, two clay pots. Following directions, I added water frequently and fertilized once a month. If the trees grew too fast, the directions assured me, I could simply prune them back to the desired height. With all my fine care, I was smug I'd soon be standing under trees twice my height, holding pruning shears and saying, "I told you so" to my skeptical husband.

When we transplanted ourselves to Georgia, a bare and treeless lawn welcomed us. Our first summer here we traveled to a nearby nursery and purchased three fast-growing Leyland cypress trees and two magnolias that I hoped would one day provide summer shade as the huge magnolias had at Grandma Watts' Woodstation home. As predicted, the

Leyland cypress shot up, but the magnolias, although quick to bear sweet-scented white blooms, took their time growing. Three years after being planted, the magnolias remained almost as short as I.

So, the Poo-Pahs were exactly what we needed—quick growing, beautiful, and easy. Like the ad said, "Simply add water … stand back … and watch it zoom!" I envisioned grabbing an iced tea, sitting on the porch, and watching it zoom until it brushed the clouds. I contemplated the concept of tall things—trees and skyscrapers, for example—that fascinate us. Is it because they are closer to heaven than we mere humans? Or is it the idea that something that starts out so small can turn into something so gigantic? Could that be why Jack traded in the family cow for a beanstalk?

While I pondered theories of human attraction to height, my delicate Royal Poo-Pah seedlings loafed around in their pots. Following directions, I kept them inside, out of extreme heat. I daydreamed of lavender blooms that would make me the envy of neighbors, even the green thumb couple down the lane with 16 hardwood trees in their yard. (But who's counting?)

By late summer, the plants had zoomed to a mighty 11 inches in their pots, about nine inches taller than when they had arrived. When the weather cooled, before the first frost, I called upon my lawn and landscape man, Brett, to come dig two holes for the seedlings, instructing him to leave plenty of room for the soon-to-be 30-foot canopy. He looked quizzically at the plants.

"I think you might have yourself a cottonwood," he said.

"But I paid for a Royal Poo-Pah," I protested.

"Cottonwoods are good," he laughed.

Later, Brett did some research and found out that although the seedlings looked like cottonwoods, my trees were in fact a different species. My Poo-Pahs and cottonwoods are often mentioned in the same breath because they are considered two of the fastest growing trees in the eastern US.

"The eastern cottonwood is native to the area, but your tree, the Royal Empress, was introduced from China," Brett said. "It'll look beautiful in bloom. I think you picked a good one!"

I felt better hearing a professional confirming my choice, but by late October, the leaves had fallen off my now 12-inch "trees" leaving two bare sticks poking up in our lawn.

All normal, said the directions. The roots would remain alive underground, and new growth would appear in the spring.

When it snowed, looking at the pitiful sticks, I found it hard to believe they would ever grow again. In late March, I saw tender green leaves curling out from one of the sticks. In mid-April, when the seedlings were a year old, they had zoomed to 24 inches. Surely a full year would count as a "season," so where were the other 10 feet the ad suggested?

Perhaps I was overly optimistic to believe my mail-order trees would grow as fast as summer corn, or Jack's beanstalk. With warm weather here, I expect big things out of my trees. Legendary growth. If those Poo-Pahs don't start shooting up soon, I just might have to trade them in for some magic beans.

A giant beanstalk in our front yard would be much taller than our cypress trees, even grander than those 16 hardwoods down the road. Or I could harvest those magic beans to sell. Who knows? I might even decide to advertise my magic beans in a magazine and give those Royal Poo-Pah folks some competition.

THE OLD SWIMMING HOLE

Georgia, 1920s-1960s

Only one thing would cause a perfectly sane person to plunge into a snaky, muddy creek: a sweltering day in Georgia.

When I was growing up, I was one of many who found relief in the local swimming hole down in Woodstation that was called "The Keyes Swimming Hole" after the family who owned the property for many years. Located on the Little Chickamauga Creek, the swimming hole was a popular gathering spot as early as the 1920s, according to Mildred Coulter Capehart, a lifelong resident.

"The Keyes went there, and others would join them," she said. She and her eight sisters and two brothers frequented the creek—but not in bathing suits.

"You wore regular clothes, like overalls," said Mildred. "The creek would get muddy, and your clothes would end up being muddy, too."

The creek's allure was especially strong for those who toiled in the fields, as did Harry Watts, my late uncle. His wife, Barbara Trundle Watts, shared the story of a scorching summer day that found Harry raking hay with a team of horses not far from the creek.

"He got hot and tied up the horses and jumped in the creek to cool off. When he came out of the creek, the horses spooked when they saw him. He chased after the horses and managed to stop them. When he returned home, Harry's father said, 'What happened over there in the field? We looked out across the field and saw that hay rake bouncing up and down."

Barbara first visited the swimming hole at the age of 15 when her family, the Trundles, moved to Woodstation. She didn't swim much, but later married Harry Watts, my father's brother. He carved their initials in a tree near the swimming hole. Her friend, Sue Capehart Gracy, remembers swimming in the creek on July 4th, the day Barbara and Harry married.

"It must have been 110 degrees that day. Grady Trundle, Barbara's father, and his brother Bob rounded up a bunch of us kids, and we went down to the swimming hole to cool off. I ended up going to Barbara's wedding with wet hair."

On another occasion, Sue was walking down a dirt road on the way to the swimming hole when she and Evelyn Keyes were confronted by an angry bull.

"We ran all the way back to escape," she said. "And then we had to figure out a different way to get to the swimming hole."

Local children went through a rite of passage down at the creek.

"I was eight or nine and my brothers and sisters threw me in," said Jeanette Williams Wilbanks, a Woodstation resident. "The water wasn't real deep, but to a child it was. When I climbed out of the creek, my big brother Ronald assured me he wouldn't have let me go under."

Charles Trundle also learned to sink or swim at the creek when he was six. A teenager, Bill Watts (my late uncle), threw him in and yelled out, "Swim or drown."

"Of course, he would have rescued me, but I did learn to swim," said Charles. According to Charles, the creek had several man-made improvements. "The creek was dynamited to make it deeper, and then Eddie Childers and Dave Hooper rigged a rope trolley that ran from one tree to another across the creek. They put in diving boards, and there was a swinging rope that hung from a tall tree across the creek."

The creek attracted kids, teens, and entire families. Access to the creek was on a dirt road that ran from near the bridge on West Nickajack through the fields. Verna Watts Bible said she remembers driving across the field to the creek in her dad's truck when she was growing up in the 1960s.

"As we got closer to the creek, I'd smell the earthy, damp smell of the creek. Then I'd see the clothes spread out all over the bushes where people had shed their clothes and jumped in wearing their shorts or bathing suits." Verna was always glad when she saw a big crowd there.

"I loved it when there were a lot of people because then there weren't any snakes," she said. "What was scary was the things that brushed up against your legs when you stepped into the creek. Probably fish, or weeds, but I always heard there were water moccasins or copperheads down there."

On the weekends, the creek was the place to be, a community gathering spot.

"Everybody came," said Dean Watts (my brother). "All the locals were there sunbathing on towels, like they do at the beach. Many brought picnic lunches." Dean recalled riding through the field, tying his horse to a tree, and jumping in the creek on a hot day.

"The creek was muddy, but it was nice and cool," said Dean.

No one remembers exactly when, but the swimming hole became less popular. Many of the locals started going to pools instead, and to the Ringgold Swimming Pool built in 1964.

Today, the area where sunbathers once spread their towels is overgrown with tall grass and bushes. There are no diving boards. A few years ago, a flood washed away the top half of the tree that once held a rope swing.

High waters may one day claim that ragged tree stump, but not the memories. Today, the swimming hole, and the adventures belong to the beavers, fish, turtles, and snakes who make this place their home.

NOT JUST LUCK

Georgia, 2015

Did you ever hear the Stone Soup story? I first heard it on Captain Kangaroo, a children's TV show, and later I read the book, "Stone Soup," by Marcia Brown. In this tale, three famished soldiers convince the townspeople to contribute to their stone soup. First they ask for a large pot and water, and then three smooth stones. A fire is built under the pot in the village square. Then the soldiers request a few more items—salt, pepper, cabbage, carrots, potatoes, and a little meat. Everyone in town contributes something, and eventually, a tasty soup fit for a king is ready to eat, enough for everyone to share.

The stone soup story reminds me of our Southern custom of potlucks, also known as covered dish, on the ground, or pot blessing. By sharing what we have, we come together for an entire meal—usually.

Participating in a potluck can be riskier than stone soup because you just don't know what you're going to get. On one occasion I walked into a potluck dinner to see a spread that was mostly desserts—heavily frosted cakes, tall pies, and creamy banana puddings. On that particular evening very few cooks had bothered to make hearty casseroles, savory green beans, turnip greens, or crispy fried okra, my favorites.

When I first moved back to the South, I was confounded by the demands of cooking for frequent potlucks. Once or twice a month, I was required to bring a dish to some social event. I needed some ideas, so I consulted my South Georgia cousin.

"Just buy those frozen meatballs, a jar of grape jelly, a jar of barbecue sauce, and toss them into a crock pot for a few hours," she said. "Everyone will love them." Sure, they would—but then they'd keel over from all the sweetness. I just couldn't bring myself to do that to friends.

Although I appreciated my cousin's suggestion, I gleaned my bookshelf and rediscovered a cherished recipe book, the Woodstation United Methodist Church Cookbook published around 1983 or 1984. Flipping through, I found classic potluck dishes I'd enjoyed growing up, squash and broccoli casseroles, baked hams, and chow chow relish. Many of my favorites were contributed by beloved family members and friends.

After choosing a dish and gathering the list of ingredients, I placed the open recipe book on the counter, so I could follow the instructions as I worked. Reading the words written by one of my late aunts, I could almost hear her voice talking to me right there in my kitchen. I could imagine how she must have enjoyed preparing this dish for our family gatherings, one of which was the annual homecoming dinner laid out on wooden tables in Grandma Watts' orchard that spanned out over the field in front of her home. In the 1950s and 1960s, many of those dishes were made with fresh vegetables and fruits grown by neighbors on their own farms.

As much as I like to reminisce, these days I enjoy homecoming in our air-conditioned, mosquito-free church hall. As a frequent potlucker, I've learned a few things that I'd like to share.

- When approaching the spread and an array of dishes, look it over and decide which dishes you want to sample. It's best to take only a small portion of each item. Why? This way you can "sample" each thing and leave some for those behind you. Note: this rule applies to all foods except fried okra, in which case it's each man, woman, or child for himself.

- As hungry as you are, do not go back for seconds until everyone else (including the kitchen helpers) has had their first plate.
- When sitting at the table and within earshot of others, only say nice things about any particular dish you are eating. After all, the creator of that dreadful gray meat concoction could be sitting next to you.
- And speaking of concoctions, at potlucks, colorful jello and marshmallow creations are called "salads."
- When you prepare something for a potluck, put it in a labeled, unremarkable serving dish or pot. I once lost an expensive blue boiler at a potluck, a gourmet double-handled designer beauty. It was my fault—I did not have a label on my pot!
- Bring a dish that you'll enjoy, one that won't spike your sugar levels into the next universe. By doing this, you'll be assured of something good to eat.
- As in life, you increase your "luck" at a potluck by making an effort. After all, if everyone had contributed only stones

to the pot, it wouldn't have turned out to be such a tasty soup.

Turnip Greens

A recipe from Aunt Margaret Morgan Watts

½ peck turnip greens water (enough to cover)

¼ lb. seasoning meat or ham hock

Other kinds of greens cook the same way.

Wash and cook greens; remove any objectionable parts of stems. Bring meat and water to a boil; add greens and bring to a hard boil. Lower heat and cook slowly for two hours or until tender.

A VISIT FROM THE VET

Georgia, 2016

On the last day of the year, while other folks were out buying their collards and black-eyed peas, or primping for New Year's Eve parties, Steve and I were out in the round pen with our three horses waiting for the veterinarian's arrival.

It had all started the week before when my mare, Fancy, started choking on her oats. She tried to cough them out and ended up lying down on the ground and rolling around as I watched. I was sure she was about to die (she's 23). Remarkably, after a few minutes, she stood up again and successfully coughed out all the oats. I telephoned our vet and was told to keep an eye on her. If it happened again, I needed to have her checked.

A few days later, another choking episode occurred, but this time it was Sunny, our red gelding, who choked on his oats. He immediately stopped eating and coughed his feed out in a less dramatic fashion, no rolling required. Seeing a pattern, I had a hunch the horses' teeth might be the culprit. Several years before, the vet suggested it was time to "float" (file down) the horse's teeth, and I'd put it off for the last five years, figuring I'd get around to it about the time I got the money to purchase a manure vacuum or construct a climate-controlled barn, both on my bucket list. Besides, my father never had dental work done on any of our many horses. They all lived to ripe old ages. Of course, that was back in the 1960s, so perhaps routine dental maintenance for horses was now a requirement, just as it is for dogs. Not so cheap if you have three horses.

Dr. White arrived carrying his tool kit, which in this case included a large, scary device that looked like something more suitable for Hannibal Lecter in *The Silence of the Lambs*. This metal speculum would be put into the horse's mouth to leave it propped open while the vet checked its teeth, after he gave her a sedative. He pulled out a long syringe and gave Fancy an intravenous dose of drugs that had her drowsy within minutes. As soon as the drugs kicked in, her head hung low, and she looked like she'd had one too many.

"She's not too bad," he said, peering inside her mouth. He pulled out a long metal file and began filing down teeth that had sharp points. He rinsed her mouth with a blue antiseptic, and after 20 minutes or so, he was done. He removed the speculum and let her loose to wander around the pen in a daze.

Next up was our gelding. The whole process was repeated, except Sunny, a big old boy, received a higher dose of sedatives and looked like a drunken sailor by the time it was over. He staggered away and wandered over to the hay rack. He grabbed a clutch of hay in his mouth but then just stood there holding it in his teeth, apparently falling asleep mid-bite.

I led Bianca up for her exam. Dr. White didn't think anything was wrong with her; the only way to find out was to give her a sedative and put on the Hannibal Lecter mask. The decision was ours.

"Let's do it," I said. "After all, you're already here." Ca Ching.

The vet gave her a strong dose of sedative, and soon her mouth was wide open. Dr. White ran his fingers along her teeth, pulled his hand out, and tossed something into the bucket of antiseptic water.

"That was a loose tooth," he said. "Just sitting there waiting to fall out." He found another loose tooth and pulled it out, and then began filing as he talked. "Her teeth are bad." Whereas the file had glided somewhat smoothly over the first two horses' teeth, it now made a racket as the vet worked on grinding down sharp points.

"I guess I should have checked her teeth when we went to get her," I said, referring to the time we acquired Bianca several years ago from her previous owners. She looked healthy and was "free."

Bianca's dental work took the longest time, but finally Dr. White pulled off the dental bridle. She staggered away to join the others while the vet explained that she'd need more regular dental exams.

"Her teeth are widely spaced, and crooked. More likely to get food particles trapped in-between." I nodded as I signed the check, noting the amount was large enough to buy collards, black-eyed peas, and several cases of French champagne.

As I waved him goodbye and New Year's Eve approached, I pondered what it all meant. I was left with a dwindling bank account, three drunken horses, and two discolored horse molars. Could I sell the teeth to be worn as jewelry or put them under my pillow and fool the tooth fairy? If you're interested, I'll cut you a deal.

I'll never forget the last day of 2015 or the valuable lesson I learned. Next time someone offers me a "gift" horse, I'm looking in its mouth!

LIFE LESSONS FROM HORSES

Georgia, 2015

Have you ever seen those bumper stickers "Ask me about my honor student?" If I had a bumper sticker on my car, it would read "Ask me about my horses."

All my horses arrived at my farm without operating instructions, and in some cases plenty of "baggage" I discovered. There are three of them: the fragile adoptee, the clown, and the aging beauty.

A trim buckskin Paso Fino mare, Bianca is my adopted horse. She had gone through many owners before ending up with an older couple who no longer wanted her. They simply had too many horses, and Bianca needed to go. When we arrived to pick her up, the woman handed me the lead rope with tears in her eyes.

"Please take good care of her, and if you don't want her, bring her back," she said. I wasn't sure why she told me this—until I got to know Bianca. This skittish mare didn't want to be caught, and ignored handfuls of carrots, apples, and other treats. She was beautiful but hard to love. I kept trying. After a few weeks, and with great coaxing, I was able to get her to eat out of my hand, and eventually she let me pet her, then catch her. When my husband tried to catch her, she pulled away. When he wore a hat, her eyes widened, and she dashed off. If I made a sudden movement around her, she jerked away as though she expected to be hit. From her behavior, we speculate that earlier in her life, she was abused by a man wearing a hat. After two years of working with her, one day she finally showed her complete trust in me by lying down in my presence. I was shocked and thrilled. All my patient work had paid off.

Our Sunny came to us through an auction where we were the highest bidders. This easy red Quarter Horse moved into our pasture, settling in quickly and acting as though he owned the place. From his previous owner we learned he had lived on a ranch in a large herd of horses. Noting several of his busted-out teeth, we figure he had been kicked by some of his herd mates. And from the way he can stop on a dime and turn quickly, we imagine he was used to round up cattle or other horses at some point. When you try to mount him, he starts backing up like a roping horse will when a calf has been lassoed.

He is an affable fellow, for the most part. On occasion, he tries to dance sideways through a Sunday afternoon ride. Either he simply wants to have fun, or he's trying to see what he can get away with. He's always clowning around. He has removed hats from our heads and unlocked gates. He likes to steal the other horses' food. Most everyone likes Sunny.

Just after moving here, we traveled to Rockmart to pick out our American bulldog puppy. In the field next to the kennels, a dark beauty grazed. Seeing me, she lifted her head and made eye contact. We had an instant connection.

I was told Fancy was a Quarter Horse, Arab cross, and 12, but later learned from my vet that she was probably a Morgan and 15. None of this mattered. Whatever she was, I wasn't going to take her back. I was smitten.

We didn't have much information about her background. From the way she holds her head up when she walks, and the way she stretches out in the paddock when tied up, I am sure she was shown as a younger horse. She was also at one time a mother, according to the vet. She is mostly a loner, preferring to keep her distance from the other horses.

With her chronic laminitis (foundering), she has bouts of lameness and has on four occasions been expected not to recover. Every go-round, we've nursed her through. She always bounces back in a few weeks to trot off with her head held high. Her spirit is strong, and because of this, she survives.

Fancy is my most huggable horse. If you throw your arms around her neck and put your cheek up against her mane, she will stand still as you share your troubles. It's as though she knows what you're saying. One friend calls her an old soul. I think of Fancy as a wise old woman.

Each of my horses has a backstory that affects its behavior. I may never know exactly what happened with their previous owners. I only see how each horse acts out in front of me.

I try to remember this fact when encountering people I've never met, particularly those who seem curt or off-putting. I don't really know what someone has been through, what baggage they are carrying. I don't know how rough or easy their lives have been before the moment we meet. I try to think of my horses and the lessons they have taught me. Be kind, be patient. Keep an open heart, or at least try.

REFLECTIONS ON TORNADO

Georgia, 2016

Where were you April 27, 2011 when the tornado first touched down in Catoosa County on Davis Ridge? I was about five miles south, standing on my back porch searching the sky for an approaching funnel, but seeing instead the slender pine trees in my yard bow down to forceful winds.

A few minutes later, the tornado slammed into Ringgold at 150 miles an hour. If you were in or near Ringgold that evening, you will most likely remember the way you felt as the tornado bore down on the town, or the way the funnel looked as it dropped down from the sky headed your way. When you recall that day, you may once again think about the roar that sounded like a train. You may have even witnessed the wind plow into the earth and churn up everything in its path. In Ringgold, darkness was punctuated with bright flashes of light as the storm created explosions in its wake.

Like nature's Godzilla, the twister was low, dark, and ugly, roiling through town to level homes, businesses, and trees, uprooting lives in the process. Eight people lost their lives that day in Ringgold, and a Ringgold High student died in the tornado as it touched down in Ooltewah. Afterward, Ringgold looked like it had been bombed. Some 30 businesses were demolished and 40 or more were damaged. Between 75-100 homes were damaged or destroyed with the worst damage inflicted on Cherokee Valley Road where 12 homes were leveled. On Highway 151 at exit 348, the tornado destroyed the Super 8 Motel, the McDonald's, a Taco Bell, and several gas stations. Churches were destroyed or damaged, along with the Catoosa County Department of Family and Children Services and other businesses on Nashville Street in downtown Ringgold. Ringgold High School and Ringgold Middle School were both severely damaged.

We grieved first for the victims and their families. Later, we mourned the loss of places, some never to be rebuilt. And for many nights after the tornado, light was absent in the main corridor that is Highway 151, normally lit up with an array of colorful signs.

With no electricity and no TV the day after the tornado, I had no idea of the extent of the destruction. Traveling along the back roads, my son and I drove up to check on my mother-in-law, passing by downed power lines and uprooted trees. Law enforcement had closed off the 151 corridor, so we decided to join a crowd of others walking down Boynton Drive to observe the damage from afar. Standing near the Holiday Inn Express, I held my mother-in-law's hand, and we looked at the mangled topsy-turvy world that the day before was fast food restaurants. I felt shaky inside. As disconcerting as it was, I was glad to be alive.

Ringgold fought back, recovered, and rebuilt—for the most part. Eventually, Ringgold Middle School and High School both reopened. Inviting lights once again lined Highway 151 at nighttime, promising food, fuel, or a comfortable bed for those passing by. Many buildings have been repaired or rebuilt and some relocated, but others never came back. There is no longer a Chow Time or a Ruby Tuesday. The friendly couple who ran a drugstore in the Food Lion Shopping Center never rebuilt. And there are others.

Even though it has been only five years, I now have trouble remembering where some places used to be. On a recent visit to the rebuilt Waffle House, I pulled out of the parking lot and right over a curb that shouldn't have been there, the outline of a building that is no longer there. This now blank space is a cement area with a curb perimeter tall enough to knock a car out of alignment. Since I could not remember what was there before the tornado, I asked a server at the Waffle House if she remembered. She said it was a motel.

Although the town looks "normal" again, I'm not sure I've quite recovered. When strong winds come through, and particularly at times when tornado warnings are issued, I feel vulnerable. On windy nights, I lie awake and listen to the sounds. The wind grows stronger, louder, like a train approaching the station but not slowing down. How close is it? I ponder all of this while reciting my favorite verse, the 23rd Psalm. It helps.

Sometimes the noise from the wind is so loud that I consider getting in the closet to wait for the storm. I weigh that option against a night of trying to get some sleep while lying amidst an uneven landscape of shoes, tennis balls, and empty duffel bags. I tell myself, "It'll probably pass over, and I won't blow away." I hope.

In a few more years, I may not remember what buildings were where before the tornado hit, yet I'll never forget the smell of upturned earth and the sight of buildings with their innards all a tangle.

No matter how many years come and go without another tornado, I will never forget that April evening. On days when dark clouds loom low and nights when the wind plays her hand, I will stay vigilant. And I will always listen for the roar.

DIESEL AND GRITS

"Down here in Georgia a man runs on diesel and grits."

—said by a gentleman farmer reading his

tractor manual over a bowl of buttery grits

Georgia, 2014

At harvest time, you get stuck behind them on the highway. You may own one yourself. There are little ones, which I call riding lawnmowers, one of which was the subject of a movie called *The Straight Story* where a man drove his mower on a 300-mile road trip. And there are big ones, the type that comes in handy when high grass needs haying, or cockleburs need to be slashed into submission.

Instead of buying a pricey John Deere (the Mercedes-Benz of the tractor world), we decided to get a used one. Ours is an antique of sorts, a 65-horsepower Case, Harvester

International (H.I.) made in the 1970s. A friend steered us to this affordable, allegedly reliable, diesel-fueled beast of a machine.

Trouble is our tractor needs a lot of coaxing to start up. We've thought about holding a prayer meeting around the machine, but what really seems to work is ether infusions—if we happen to have some on hand.

On the rare occasion the thing runs, my gentleman farmer husband worries about how much work it can handle. Referring to the tractor as "she," he says things like, "I'd hate to kill her pulling this fallen tree," and "she's too old to pull up that stump." At other times, he's described her as elegant and powerful and "quirky." When I look puzzled at some of his descriptions, he says Harvester International aficionados would get it. I don't.

Seasons come and seasons go, and she sits in the field shamelessly surrounded by tall grass, weeds, and sometimes snow. Amie, the barn cat, has figured out a use for the tractor. She claws her way up the grooved tires to perch high above the tall grass and watch the world—and potential prey—go by. A very pricey kitty perch.

With major bush hogging begging to be done, my husband decided this spring to get the tractor fixed once and for all.

"It'll be pricey," he said. "But more economical than getting a new one."

The elegant and powerful beast had to be hauled in on a trailer—in our case our friend's—also named Steve—to get to the tractor doctor. After a few days of checking it over, the mechanic recommended a long list of fixes: glow plugs ("glow little glow worm glow"), injectors, and other parts. My Steve agreed to the repairs.

We waited and watched the summer grass and weeds continue their growth spurts unabated. A few weeks later, the two Steves returned to pick up the tractor. The first mechanic recommended further repairs by a different mechanic, one who specializes in alternators, batteries, and starters. That took another two weeks.

After the second round of repairs, the two Steves returned our tractor to our pasture, which now looked like a jungle.

"Great," I said. "So, can we do that bush hogging tomorrow?" Steve shook his head no.

"I need to get an air filter and replace grease filters, and lubricate," he said. Another delay requiring two more trips to the auto supply store.

One sunny Saturday, a full two months after the initial push to get the tractor fixed, it was show time. The dog, cat, and I stood in the tall grass watching and waiting. My husband climbed aboard the rusty squeaky seat and turned the key. The engine jumped to life with a roar. Steve let her warm up for a while just to be sure it wasn't a false start. I asked him when he was going to hook up the bush hog.

"Not today," he said. "Not until I get a three-point hitch control arm."

The whole tractor repair process reminds me of a tricky SAT word problem. "If the tractor repair costs as much as three horses' oats and hay for six months, is it cheaper to buy a mule?" My answer is this: With the amount of money we spent, a mule would have been a bargain. Admittedly, mules are stubborn, and so is our tractor.

The X factor in this problem is that Steve loves his tractor, just like a lot of folks down here, as reflected in T-shirt slogans such as, "Tractors never die" and "Will trade husband for tractor."

Which leads to another question. Would you trade your significant other for a tractor? A fancy, new green one with an air-conditioned cab and 120 horsepower? I wouldn't. I'd rather have my husband than a tractor, or a mule for that matter. He roars to life with coffee, not ether, and doesn't require a lot of costly repairs. If he ever does, I won't need a flatbed trailer to haul him.

The main problem is that if I traded him for a new tractor, he wouldn't be around to operate the thing. Although I can cook a mean pot of grits, I don't know the first thing about diesel. So, I'll keep the quirky antique one, the Case, H.I. tractor I mean, and my husband, too, thank you very much.

A NOT SO FISHY TALE

Tennessee, 2004

Everyone has a fish story to share, and I am no exception, but mine's not really about the fish. Let me explain.

Before we ever moved to Georgia from California, my big brother Dean, a whitewater river guide, talked us into a fishing trip on the Tellico River in Tennessee. Dean swore the trout would leap for the hooks as soon as we tossed in the lines. We would arrive first and settle in, and a few days later he'd drive up and see us. In the meantime, we would explore on our own.

Arriving at our cabin, we passed other guests who were already sitting on their cabin porches and taking in the view of the river. We unloaded our bags into our bare bones cabin. Soon the sun would set, so Steve and Jack grabbed their poles and tackle box.

"They'll be hitting now," my husband said. He and Jack started to head out of the cabin's back door, across the back porch, and to the river, which lay a hundred yards away.

"Wait," I said. "Don't forget the bug repellent." All three of us sprayed our legs, arms, and necks. "Now those mosquitoes can't get us," I said.

"Want to come with us?" Steve asked.

"Sure," I answered, grabbing a novel and my little notebook and pen I always carry along to record details when I travel. We walked across a lawn toward the river. Steve gestured toward the grass.

"This might be more comfortable than sitting on those rocks by the river."

"I think so," I said. "I'll be right here." I perused the grass, which was coarse-looking and probably would feel itchy if I hadn't been wearing jeans. Then I saw a sandy spot. Lovely! Just like a California beach, but by a river. How lucky was I? I would feel right at home. I sat down and pulled out my novel. The lowering sun bathed me in light as I found my place in the book. Things couldn't get any better.

Suddenly, I felt hot, stinging thorns all over my bottom. I jumped up and yelled for help.

"I sat in some nettles!" I screamed. Steve turned and looked at me. By now, I was hopping up and down like a Mexican jumping bean. He ran toward me with Jack trailing him. "Ow! Ow! Get the nettles out!"

Then Steve was behind me and quickly assessing the situation.

"Pull your pants down!" he ordered. I hesitated. We were out in the wide open within plain view of the cabins, not to mention our son. "Now!" he yelled. I pulled my jeans down around my ankles and waited for him to pull out the nettles. Instead, he started brushing and slapping my underside.

"What are you doing?" I cried as I tried to wiggle out of range.

"Stand still!" he ordered. "It's ants!" On the verge of tears, I stood motionless as one can while being stung by fire ants and brush-slapped at the same time. At that moment, I had a good idea of how Dante felt in his journey through hell.

After the ants were off, I pulled my jeans back up—cautiously, I might add—over the still stinging area. We headed back to the cabin. Steve told me to lie down on the bed so he could treat the bites with witch hazel. He dabbed the bites with cool, wet cotton balls and a light touch. Even so, each dab stabbed like fire.

"How many are there?" I asked.

"Fifty, at least," he answered. No wonder I was feeling numb and dizzy. Could I be having an allergic reaction?

For obvious reasons, for the next 12 hours, I lay on my stomach reading and sleeping. By the next morning, I was sore, and the bites had turned into reddish blisters. I forced myself to get up and move around. I didn't want to ruin our trip, so when my husband and son drove upstream along the road that parallels the river, I lay on my side in the back seat. Finding a comfortable position was challenging.

Upon our return home, I visited my allergist and found out that I could have had a serious reaction to the stings. Some have difficulty breathing, throat swelling, and a rapid heartbeat. He warned me that the next time I was stung by several fire ants, or by one fire ant several times (the ants can sting multiple times), I could have a more severe reaction. Some people are actually allergic to the venom, and deaths have been reported. Children and pets are the most vulnerable.

Unfortunately, our pasture is home to several fire ant colonies. At the water faucet the other day, a sneaky fire ant latched onto my palm. I felt a burning pain and assumed it came from a thorn or nettle until I tried to remove the "thorn" from my skin. That ant clung on. As my husband had done, I slapped it off. The bad boy fell apart and landed in pieces on the ground.

I regret I have no fish tale to share from my Tellico Plains trip, but Steve never tires of sharing his version of what happened the day I unwittingly sat in the wrong spot. We like to think of it as our "Fifty Shades of Fire Ants" moment.

SECOND STRING PLAYER

Georgia, 2012-2025

I've often written about my huggable, fluffy bay Morgan mare, Fancy, also known as my heart horse. When her health began to fail, and she could not be ridden very often due to her hoof problems, I searched for a back-up horse, or as I like to say, "a second-string player." A friend told me of a Paso Fino mare, well-trained, needing a new home. She was 12.

Bianca was her name, and I had encountered her before. Two years earlier, this trim buckskin was up for adoption, but she could not be caught. Not even her owner at the time could catch her. As we drove away, I said to my husband, "I don't want to be with any horse that doesn't want to be with me." She was as wary as our feral barn cat.

Fate had different plans. She was once again up for adoption. I hesitated, but my Fancy's laminitis was getting worse. Clearly, it was time to give Bianca another try. When we arrived at the pasture about half an hour away, Bianca was running with a herd of five, including one that was her yearling colt trying to nurse. Her hooves were long and curling up, a sign she'd not been trimmed in a long time, most likely because she could not be caught! My cowboy friend Winston pulled out a bucket of feed and a rope and began to lure her into roping range. She finally succumbed to the sweet smell of feed, or maybe it was Winston's cowboy charm. Within minutes, Winston roped her and loaded her into the trailer and headed to our farm.

I got my first real look at her when she backed out of the trailer. A bag of skin and bones, but with potential. Her buckskin coat looked like heavily creamed coffee, with black mane and tail and boots. With our lush pasture and plenty of feed, I aimed to fatten her up. First, I had to catch her.

But this second-string player wanted no part of being caught or ridden. It would take time to build her trust. I rattled the feed bucket and lured her to the trough with no ulterior motive. Eventually, she allowed me to pet her, and occasionally I succeeded in catching her. This process took months and tested my patience.

Once bridled and saddled, she was a dream to ride. Her gait reminded me of a slow gate or rack from my days growing up riding a five-gaited horse. When she moved into her "small steps" mode, we glided through the fields, my head not moving at all as she performed her fancy footwork.

Watching from the wings, or rather from the round pen where she rested during her many battles with laminitis, my Fancy looked wistful as we zipped away. I missed her, of course, but my second-string player was a smooth horse and obeyed every command. I had lucked out.

As the years passed and Fancy's condition worsened, I spent more and more time riding Bianca, but still with torn allegiance. I divided my pasture time with petting and tending to Fancy, which sometimes included wetting her hay or soaking her sore feet, and riding Bianca.

I could see Fancy was uncomfortable with her sore hooves, and her condition grew to the point that she would no longer tolerate her hooves being trimmed. The final straw came when she tried to "sit" down on the horse trimmer.

"I can't work with her anymore," said the trimmer, "unless you bring in a hoist to lift her from the ground next time. She is leaning into me because the pain is so bad."

"I don't have a truck with a hoist," I said.

"Then you'll have to borrow one or rent one. I cannot risk getting hurt. I'm sorry." She started to put away her tools.

"Is it time to put her down?" I asked.

"If you can't get her hooves taken care of, you might want to think about it." And I did. It was time. I called the vet to set up a time.

A light rain fell on the day when the veterinarian arrived. She asked me if I was sure. I wasn't sure I was ready, but I knew Fancy was. She had suffered for five years with laminitis, far too long. As the vet gave her the first injection, a sedative, I stood next to her head and petted her on the neck. I spoke to her.

"It's okay, girl," I said as she started to nod off. I stroked her smooth coat.

"Stand back, she's going to fall down!" said the vet. Fancy's knees buckled, and she crumpled down on her side. The vet gave her the final injection. I crouched down next to her head and spoke to her, trying to comfort her. Her legs moved as if she were running. Galloping to horse heaven, I thought.

And then she was gone. The vet listened to her heart, no longer beating. I stroked her neck as the tears coursed down my cheeks, diluted by raindrops now coming down in a steady drizzle. I lay down and put my head on her neck and wept. Steam rose from her still warm body. My husband telephoned the grave digger.

I mourned my Fancy for many months, even bought a custom gravestone with her picture etched on it and the phrase, "A good and gentle horse. Your spirit lives on." I planted daffodil bulbs beside the grave.

I could not mourn too long; other horses needed care, my husband's horse, and Bianca. My second-string player was now first string, a fact she seemed to sense. She approached me when I came into the pasture, seeking out feed and treats.

I kept thinking of reasons not to like her as much as Fancy. Her ears were too long, her tail was not full enough, and she wasn't as fluffy as Fancy. Still, she was well-trained and never tried to bolt off while I was mounting her. Her gait was smooth as we glided through the fields. Slowly, I began to focus on her good qualities. She was not my huggable Fancy. She was different, and yet she behaved better.

The daffodils on Fancy's grave bloomed spring after spring. Sadly, Steve's Quarter Horse caught an equine parasite. Despite thousands of dollars of treatment, he had to be put down. Bianca was now our only horse, our first-string player. As Fancy had once done, Bianca now came to me and followed me all the way from the gate to the feeding area. To keep her company, we adopted a part-Mustang paint that we later discovered was blind. For several years, she kept Bianca company until she ran into a fence and was fatally injured.

On her last birthday, Bianca turned 26. The years have left their mark on my old mare. The vet pulled several teeth and at the last visit stated, "She has one tooth in her head." She has a hard time keeping the weight on, and now I (or a helper) must feed her twice a day with warm, wet senior feed to keep her from being too thin. In the chill of winter, she wears a waterproof blanket to help her stay warm and dry. On pretty days when the sun is out, we explore the pasture together and enjoy the sights and sounds of nature. Until last fall, I rode her around at a leisurely pace for a few minutes.

Now her back legs are growing frail, and she really should not carry anything larger than a child. Bianca is no longer young, and neither am I. I do not know who will outlast whom. She's stubbornly tough, but so am I. We have come full circle. She arrived as a second-string player, turned into a first-string player, and today is a last-string player. Until one of us goes, we will continue to roam the fields, enjoying one another's company.

UNEXPECTED BLOOMS

Georgia, 2013

When the thermometer had dropped to almost freezing in the nighttime, my tomato plant suddenly began blooming and bearing fruit. On evenings when below 40 was predicted, I covered my tomato plant with a light cloth, so the cold wouldn't kill my late bloomer. Winter was approaching with each passing day, but that tomato plant operated on its own timeline.

Like my tomato plant, some people flourish no matter what the season would seem to dictate. One of my friends turned 99 this autumn. Every morning, she rises and dresses herself for an eight o'clock breakfast. She does her shopping, goes to church every Sunday, and attends weddings and parties whenever she is invited. She has adapted to her physical limitations by using a walker. Her mind is perfect.

She quotes scripture by memory just as easily as she recalls the 1920s when her father drove a horse-drawn wagon to deliver ice.

When I attended the Southern Women Writers Conference after I moved back to Georgia, I met a writer who published her first novel at the age of 71. Critically acclaimed, A.J. Mayhew's novel *The Dry Grass of August* was inspired by memories of growing up in the segregated South of the U.S. It took her 18 years to write this novel, but her hard work makes this book difficult to put down once you start reading. Last I heard, she was working on another novel.

In my family, several of us have defied the expected course of our season. My mother received her B.A. at 53, at a time when most of her friends were grandmas. My uncle studied oil painting at 80 and had an exhibition of his work a few years later. In his fifties, my brother took up a paddle, donned a helmet and life jacket, and stepped into a raft and a whitewater river guiding career. More than two decades later, he's still guiding groups of rafters down class 3, 4, and 5 rapids all summer long. "I'm giving everyone a free trip when I turn 100," he says.

As for my late blooming, I took up horseback riding again in my fifties (but not without some falls) and published my first novel at a time when many of my friends were retiring. Bookselling is not for sissies. Those boxes of books weigh a lot, and it helps to have a strong back and biceps, not to mention a positive attitude.

The way I see it, we late bloomers are just time rebels. We like to do things in our own good time, not according to the calendar.

Whatever age you are—young, old, or in-between—I say there is no wrong time to bloom. Just bloom. For as Shakespeare said, "Better once than never, for never too late."

WEIGHTY WORDS

Georgia, 2013

Until my first novel was published, I didn't know how heavy words could be. Literally, I mean. My novel weighs 9.6 ounces, not even a pound. But those words add up. A box of 20 weighs 12 pounds. Combined with the weight of the box, call it 13 pounds.

Traveling alone one weekend, I arrived at the Decatur Book Festival ready to deliver my box of books. Trying to get as close as I could to the action, I pumped the parking meter with the quarters I had on hand and bought myself 24 minutes to transport my books to the right vendor area. Although early, the morning was already stifling, and as I tucked my 13 pounds of words under my arm, I realized I am not the Diana Nyad of long-distance book carrying. Plus, I had no idea where my actual destination was.

I spotted a volunteer, a woman about my age, wearing a brown Decatur Book Festival T-shirt. I asked her how to get to Pavilion "E" and explained I was on the clock.

"I'm not sure, let's find out," she said in a calm and reassuring voice. She grabbed a map, looked up the location of the pavilion, and pointed toward a spot neither of us could see, a place beyond a sea of tent tops. She tried to explain how to get there. I was clueless. Perhaps seeing my expression of complete bafflement, she said, "Why don't I take you there?"

"That would be perfect," I said. I followed her as we headed past a row of tents where book sellers were setting up. As we walked and talked, I breathed hard, sucking in the heat and humidity.

"Would you like me to carry some of your books?" she offered. Boy, would I! I popped open the lid and handed her six books. Immediately, my load felt lighter, and the distance seemed doable.

About five minutes later, when we arrived at the check-in area, there was a long line. I sighed. Certainly, my meter would run out, and I'd get a parking ticket. And I'd have to stand there holding my box of books until the line went down.

"Would you like me to wait with you?" the volunteer asked.

"If it's not too much trouble," I replied.

"Not at all," she said. While we waited, we talked. I learned her name was Brenda, and she had volunteered before. Like me, she was a big reader. She listened patiently as I voiced my worries that I would not make it back to the meter before I'd get a ticket. Finally, it was my turn to sign in. I handed over my books and turned around to try to find my way back through the maze of tents and people. Brenda offered, "Let me walk you back to where you came in."

As we walked, I told her that I really appreciated her help, that I would never have found the right tent without her assistance.

"You know, I think your being there for me is one of those God things," I said.

"I know," she said. "There's a book about that. *When God Winks at You*. It's all about coincidences," she said.

"Like me meeting you," I added. When we finally reached the festival entrance, she pointed me toward the area where I had parked my car. I thanked her and said goodbye.

I arrived back at the meter with a minute to spare. Free of the weight of my books, I could park my car in a long-term spot and walk back to the festival at a leisurely pace. I was off to a good start, all thanks to the kindness of a stranger who offered to help and to one of those winks from above.

A HAUNTING TRIP TO HISTORIC RUGBY

Tennessee, 2014

"Should you take Bella along?" Steve asked as he loaded my bags into the car for my overnight trip to Historic Rugby, Tennessee. I'd been invited there to speak as part of the Appalachian Writers Series.

"I don't think dogs are allowed where I'm staying."

"Is it a hotel?" Steve asked. As always, he was concerned about safety.

"B&B," I said. "There'll be other guests around. I'll be fine."

As I drove north on Highway 27, I was excited about seeing Rugby, an old English town built in the 1880s on the Cumberland Plateau and located just south of Big South Fork National Park. The town was founded by British author Thomas Hughes, famous for his classic novel, *Tom Brown's Schooldays*. Hughes envisioned creating a cooperative, class-free community, a place where the gentry's younger sons could build new lives through agriculture and high Christian principles. Hughes called the area "a lovely corner of God's earth."

After driving about three hours, I arrived at the Visitor's Centre. There, my host, a well-spoken Rugby resident, Jim, took me to get settled in before touring the town. Following him in my car, we drove along gravel roads through forests and past old-fashioned homes, all spaced far apart. We arrived at a large two-story Victorian house, the Newberry House. Jim carried my bag up the steep stairs and said he'd wait in the parlor for me.

Looking around the small room, I was charmed by the small writing desk and a journal that invited musings from guests. Perhaps later I'd pen something. The bed, dresser, and old pictures reminded me of my grandma's home in Woodstation, as did the smell of aged furniture polish. I snapped a few photos and then tried to call my husband to tell him I'd arrived safely. No cell phone service. I left the house to join my host for a ride around Rugby.

Jim gave me the "windshield tour" and pointed out buildings left over from the 19th century and newer reproductions. During my stay, I would visit founder Hughes' home, Christ Church Episcopal, a schoolhouse, and a working print shop. My favorite was the Victorian Library, built in 1882, which is the largest in the country with some 7,000 volumes, one of them dating to 1687.

Back at the Visitors' Centre, my cell phone finally worked, and I was able to reach Steve to tell him I had arrived safely. Then, with less than an hour till dinner, my host dropped me off at the Newbury House. When we pulled up, I noticed only one car in the parking lot. Mine. Where were the other guests? Probably out touring the town, I assumed.

I turned the key and let myself into the hallway of the 134-year-old former boarding house. I climbed the steep stairs to my room to change and study my notes. The house was very quiet—for a while. Soon, I heard voices that seemed to come from down the hall. I quickly slipped on my low heels, grabbed my presentation folder, and left the room, hoping to bump into some other guests and ask where I might get a cup of tea.

I looked down the long hallway. No one in sight. Standing at the top of the narrow stairs, I suddenly had the urge to grab the rail and hold on—so no one could push me down. What an odd thought, particularly considering I had yet to see any other people in the house.

Downstairs, I explored the parlor, replete with Victorian furnishings. Peeking behind an ample fire screen, I thought it might make the ideal place to stuff a victim. I shuddered and moved down the hall, where I found a sunroom. I tried the cell phone again. No service.

Over supper at the Harrow Road Café, Jim and his wife, Dorcus, regaled me with stories of Rugby. Turns out the early settlers were mostly wiped out by typhoid, fire, and bad weather. Some stayed on, but it was not until the early 1960s and 1970s that the town began to come alive again through the efforts of some of the townspeople.

After my book talk in the Visitor Centre, Jim and Dorcus hosted a reception for me in their home. While there, I admired a red plaque that stated, "Keep Calm and Carry On."

"It was a poster produced by the British government in World War II to raise morale," Jim explained. "Carried here at one of the shops."

"I think I'll buy one tomorrow."

For the next few hours, I mingled with the locals, an eclectic group who all loved living in Rugby. All were gracious. Several asked where I was staying.

"The Newbury House," I answered. "Does it have ghosts?"

"They won't hurt you," was the usual answer. Oh, so I hadn't imagined those voices in the empty house.

By the time Jim drove me back to the B&B, it was almost midnight. We pulled into the parking lot. Under the light cast off by a tall lamppost, I saw one car—mine.

"Where are the other guests?" I asked.

"Must have checked out," Jim replied. I looked at the empty house, its windows lit up like a jack-o'-lantern's face. It seemed to be waiting for its sole guest for the night. Me.

"Do you want me to walk you to the porch?" Jim offered.

"You can walk me in, and I can stay, but I won't sleep a wink. Not in that house, with no cell phone service, not alone." I remained seated in the car, staring at those glowing windows and contemplating a night in the creepy bedroom. Jim climbed out of the car.

"Just a minute," he said. He called his wife (*his* cell phone worked), then turned around to tell me she was making up their spare room. Did I mind cats? No, I did not. Even though I am allergic, I prefer cats to ghosts.

Once safely in Jim and Dorcus' guest room, I felt silly for being such a scaredy cat. The next morning, Jim handed me a gift from Annie, one of the shop owners. It was the red plaque I'd admired earlier.

"When I told her you liked the saying, she wanted you to have it," Jim said.

"How thoughtful," I said.

I am thinking about returning to Rugby one day to browse the shops and participate in some of the activities. There are classes in beekeeping, basket making, ornament making, yarn making, and hikes led by a naturalist. Most appealing are the late October Halloween celebrations with guided tours of Rugby's haunted past, a bonfire with cider, and storytelling.

For the adventurous wishing to make the journey to check out the Newbury House, be forewarned. You may hear other guests—the unseen kind. And if feeling unnerved, remember what that British plaque says. "Keep calm and carry on."

SPRING BREAK, CON LA FAMIGLIA

No matter what happens, travel gives you a story to tell.

—Jewish Proverb

Sicily, 2009

It was in the dead of a North Georgia winter when we came up with our "brilliant idea" for a May vacation. We would fly to Sicily to see where my husband's ancestors had come from. The "we" in this instance referred to Steve, Jack, and me, and our senior family members, my mother-in-law, her sister, and her sister's husband. My mother-in-law had always wanted to see the land where her mother and father were born, and after saving for years, we finally had enough to cover our share of the trip.

As cold days gave way to warmer ones, my plans blossomed like Bradford pears in the spring. I made plane and hotel reservations, consulted guidebooks, and obtained Euros from the bank. With this much planning, everything would go smoothly. Or not. Before we had even arrived in Sicily, we lost Uncle Charlie in the Rome, Italy, Airport.

"What were we thinking?" I asked my husband as we searched for him.

"I don't know," Steve said. Were we nuts? How would we keep track of our senior family members, all our luggage, and ourselves?

Upon our arrival in Rome, we requested a wheelchair, so Uncle Charlie wouldn't have to walk far on his bad hip. The eager, Italian-speaking wheelchair attendant whisked him away, promising to meet us once we got through customs.

After getting stuck in the elevator and escaping by crawling out halfway between floors, Steve and I went to the area where Uncle Charlie was supposed to be, but was not. Dragging our mountain of luggage behind us, we sought help at the airline counter. A lovely young attendant told us in broken English, "I take care of everything. Relax." She led us to a bench and told us to sit down.

But we could not sit. Over the next two hours, we fretted as various helpful officials telephoned around the airport trying to find our missing uncle, all the while assuring us he would soon be found. As the boarding time for the next plane neared, we reluctantly set off for the departure gate, only to find Uncle Charlie calmly waiting in the wheelchair where, he claimed, he had been for a long time.

Perhaps this one glitch was a fluke, and the trip would now go as planned, I reasoned. But once we arrived in Agrigento, Sicily, the surprises continued. Aunt Nancy had brought along her electric toothbrush but forgot a converter to make it work, and a thick stack of American dollars, but not a single Euro. We spent our first two days driving from bank to bank trying to change her money, but no one trusted Aunt Nancy, which made us all laugh. Aunt Nancy is known as a model citizen in the US.

At the hotel, after we had washed out a few dirty things, we draped wet clothes over the patio furniture to dry in the warm air. That night, the sirocco wind blew in from Africa and scattered Aunt Nancy's clothes all over the hotel's front sidewalk. The next morning at breakfast, we teased her about her "flying undies."

On a trip to buy peaches, someone slammed the rental van door shut too hard, causing the back window to shatter into little pieces all over the market parking lot. When we went to trade in the van for new wheels, we found out all they had left were two sports cars, an Alfa Romeo and a Fiat, and at the same price. Perhaps our luck was changing, and just in time for my birthday the next day.

We woke up to clear, sunny skies. I had carefully planned the day to go off without a hitch. In the morning, we would take a walking tour of "old" town Agrigento, dating from the 11th century. Our tour guide, Giovanna, warned us of the steep and winding streets and suggested the elders should stay behind. Not wanting to miss anything, young-at-heart Aunt Nancy insisted on coming anyway.

Church bells rang as we navigated our way up and down the streets, stopping to visit the Cathedral of St. Gerlando. A perfect day—until Aunt Nancy stopped at the top of a flight of stairs to point at a street sign.

"Via Romano," she said, "Like the cheese." She took a step forward into thin air and tumbled down. Motionless, she lay sprawled all over the stairs. I prayed she wasn't dead as I rushed to her side. Fortunately, nothing was broken, but her knees were bruised and bleeding. She insisted we continue our tour and even stopped along the way to buy roses for Giovanna and me. We took the shortcut back to Giovanna's house, tended to Aunt Nancy's wounds, and propped her up on the sofa with ice packs. While she rested, we returned to the hotel to retrieve the rest of the family, so they could join us for lunch.

At the hotel parking lot, we were greeted with the sight of two rearing snakes that seemed to be fighting, or dancing. Frightened, I ran inside to get the hotel owner. Upon seeing the serpents in the garden, he proclaimed, "'Tis the season of love." Ah—dancing, mating snakes. An omen?

I turned away from the snakes just in time to see Uncle Charlie fall over backwards onto the pavement. His hip had given way. My husband rushed to help him off the ground. Thankfully, he wasn't hurt, only shaken up. He decided to stay behind at the hotel and rest.

At Giovanna's home, we had a two-hour stretch with no catastrophes. Sitting at her dining room table, we enjoyed a view of the Mediterranean through the open window and a seven-course Sicilian meal she had so graciously prepared for us. We ate olives from a 2,000-year-old tree, bread, sausage, steamed artichokes, fresh strawberries, orange and fennel salad, and penne with pistachio cream sauce. Holding the grater in her hand, Giovanna asked if we'd like grated cheese on our pasta.

"Not if it's Romano," I replied. Aunt Nancy and I grinned at each other.

To celebrate my birthday, Giovanna brought out hot coffee and a strawberry and whipped cream cake topped with a fireworks candle, a Sicilian tradition. Nico, Giovanna's nine-year-old son, stepped forward to light the candle. A bright spray of flames shot up. I screamed in delight at the sight while Nico went wild, setting off poppers that rained confetti down over our heads. Even after the sparkling candle had sizzled out, the warm mood in the room remained as we lingered around the confetti-littered table sipping coffee. Finally, things seemed to be working out.

After dinner, we drove back to the hotel to take poor Uncle Charlie to get a bite. Pulling the Alfa Romeo into a restaurant parking lot, my husband accidentally sideswiped a floodlight fixture in the driveway. Three yelling Sicilian men in sauce-stained aprons ran out from the kitchen and demanded a rather large number of Euros to settle up.

Returning to the safety of my hotel room, I was greeted by a giant, wiggling millipede in our bathroom. After checking the sheets for wayward insects, I climbed into bed before something else could go wrong. I lay there thinking of the mishaps—losing Uncle Charlie in Rome, the broken car window, the falls, the broken light fixture, and the scary bug in my room—and of the good times—eating gelato, visiting the village of my husband's ancestors, and laughing together as we bumbled along foreign roadways.

Our crazy Sicily trip had turned out to be a lot like family itself, a medley of good and not-so-good, and always unpredictable. As I drifted off, my last thoughts were not of the day's disasters but of the blessing of family, firework candles, roses, Romano cheese, and yes, even those dancing snakes.

MAMA ANNE SUNSET

California, 1984

The sun was usually setting by the time I pulled up in front of my Southern California apartment after a long day at work or college where I was finishing up my master's degree. About once or twice a week, I would be surprised to spot my mother's little red Toyota parked at the curb in front of my apartment. Inside I knew I'd find "Mama Anne" and her grandson, my son Anthony, drawing with magic markers or painting with watercolors. Both enjoyed creating colorful scenes of animals, beaches, or sunsets, and sharing a few hours together. At 67, Mama was an independent sort of person who enjoyed the freedom of doing just as she pleased. Her little Toyota Corolla was just as much a part of her as a horse is to a rider, a symbol of her freedom to travel wherever she wanted.

One evening, I came home not to find my mother, but instead a message on my answering machine. In her Georgia drawl, Mama reported her whereabouts.

"Don't worry. The doctor had me check into the hospital for a few days to get over this chest infection. Don't bother driving in to come see me tonight. I'm fine. But please come get my car out of the parking lot tomorrow." That was Mama, alright. More worried about that car than herself.

A few days in the hospital turned into eight, and her condition worsened. She was transferred to ICU, where no children were allowed. The doctor told us the prospects were bad, but there was hope. "Hope springs eternal" was Mama's favorite saying. For her, I tried to remain hopeful. Anthony drew and painted cheerful scenes for me to take to her, but she said she really wanted him to come visit.

A friendly nurse helped us smuggle Anthony into the ICU to visit his grandmother. He donned a surgical mask, and we went in.

Wearing a serene smile, "Mama Anne" lay in bed surrounded by cherished drawings and paintings created by Anthony and her other grandchildren. Perhaps knowing this might be her last time seeing my son, she made a special effort to appear cheerful, although I could see she was weak.

When we returned home that day, Anthony spotted the red Toyota parked at our curb.

"Look, Mama Anne is here," he shouted. In his five-year-old mind, he assumed Mama Anne had simply checked herself out of the hospital and was once again waiting inside. He was very disappointed when I explained his aunt had simply parked the car out front, and that his grandmother was still sick.

A few days later, Mama stopped breathing, and the doctor had to put her on a respirator. I was glad she wasn't conscious because I was sure she wouldn't be happy about the respirator doing her breathing for her. She was much too independent for that.

The hours of hoping, waiting, and praying dragged on. It was late, after sundown on a Sunday, when Mama died. We went in to see her just after. She lay on her bed, clothed in white sheets and looking radiant. She no longer looked frightened but relaxed and free. Back at home, I had to tell my son.

"What does it mean that Grandma's dead?" he asked. I felt I had to be honest.

"It means that she won't ever pull up out front again in her red car, or paint pictures with us," I said. "She is in heaven now." We both cried and tried to comfort one another.

We took her south to Jackson, Georgia to bury her in her native red clay. When I returned home, I was overcome with a deep depression. Not a day went by that I did not feel the pain of Mama's death. I relived each horrible moment of her struggle to breathe. I longed to ask her if she had been in pain. I wanted to tell her how much it hurt me to see her hurting. Most of all, I wanted to tell her how much I missed coming home to find her there, painting with her grandson.

A week after the funeral, I walked on the beach alone with only my grief and several sandpipers keeping me company. Mama had so loved the sandpipers, the beach, and the sight of the sun sinking into the sea. I glanced up to look at the setting sun, a sight Mama would never witness again, I thought bitterly.

The clouds had transformed into pink cotton candy, not only to the west but to the east, north, and south. The sky was awash in shades of gold and rose. As I stared at the colorful sunset, I knew Mama was sending me a sign. My sadness lifted, and I began to feel hope again.

I have witnessed many colorful sunsets since that cold day in January. When Anthony and I see pink cotton candy clouds, we turn to one another and say, “Mama Anne” sunset. Mama lives on in heaven, painting sunsets with God.

GRATITUDE

California, 2005

A few years ago, five days before Christmas, I received the best gift of all, a thank you postcard from a woman I had never met. A month earlier, Holly, one of our church members, had organized a holiday drive to send presents to some of the congregation of a Methodist church down in Mississippi who had lost most everything after a hurricane passed through. She handed out a long list of names of children and adults requesting everything from a pair of shoes to a new bike or game. I studied the list of names and felt frustrated that I could not afford to buy something for them all, but then I remembered what Holly had said, "No gift is too small."

Scanning over the list, a name jumped out at me, a mother requesting several items for each of her three children, but only a sweater for herself. As I looked at her name and the names of her children, I was reminded of the emergency instructions given by flight attendants before take-off. "Pull down the oxygen mask and place it over your nose and mouth first, then help any small children who may be traveling with you." I felt strongly that these instructions also applied to this mother of three young children. If I could do something to help her, perhaps it would give her a boost, so she could better help her children.

I went online and found a fetching teal green sweater that would be shipped to her church from a national retailer. I hit the "order completed" button, printed out the receipt, and went about my own preparations for Christmas. In the back of my mind, I wondered when she would receive the sweater and if she would like it. I hoped it fit and was the right color. Would she like the hip-length style I had chosen? In the hectic days as Christmas neared, when there was always too much to do and not enough time, I kept this woman tucked away in the corner of my mind. I stopped and visited her there, imagining her surprise when she opened her package and found something for herself.

But six days before Christmas, all thoughts of her and my holiday preparations disappeared when our beloved 13-

year-old chihuahua passed away in the middle of the night. The joy of the season was replaced with grief for our little friend, who no longer occupied his spot in front of the fireplace ringed with a string of twinkling white lights. His death was one of many my family and friends had experienced during the past year. Holiday cheer turned into sad thoughts as I remembered everyone who would not be around to celebrate. What was the point of even trying to celebrate when I felt so empty? I went to bed with hopes that Christmas would soon come and go and that I could simply get through it. Bah humbug.

The next day, a stack of letters came through the mail slot, landed on the bare hardwood floor, where no dog growled or barked at the mailman as in days gone by. I absent-mindedly shuffled through the mail until I saw it: a handwritten card with a Mississippi postmark. A thank-you note from the mother down south. "Hi, Sweetie," she started out. She wrote that she had received the beautiful sweater and almost cried when she saw it was shipped from Kansas, where she had been born. Touching the sweater was almost like touching the green, green grass of home. I knew what she meant: I too, missed the green of the southeast where I had grown up. As I read her words, I thought of her childhood in the country, and of my own. I felt I knew her, and I had a strong connection with this woman I had never met. My spirits lifted as I thought of her wearing her warm teal sweater, surrounded by her thoughts of green. I wanted to thank her for the gift she had given me, her lovely, eloquent words that caused me to reflect on a place we both knew so well, a place where both of us would always feel safe. Home.

EMPTY NEST REFILLED

California, 2003

"Pew—eee! Come smell my knee!" my son, Jack, said. What an odd request, I thought, but I moved toward my 19-year-old, lying on the sofa with his left knee covered in thick bandages. Three days earlier he'd had reconstructive knee surgery.

"What is it?" I asked, squatting down next to the sofa.

"Just smell it, please." His voice rose to a plea. "I think maybe something's wrong." I leaned and sniffed or tried to. My nose was stuffy.

"I don't smell anything," I said.

"Of course not," he said. "You couldn't smell a rotten fish, Mom."

"Well, why did you ask me then? Never mind. What does it smell like?"

"Like someone stepped in dog …"

"Okay, I get it. Don't be so dramatic," I replied. My larger-than-life Jack has a tendency to overstate things occasionally, but perhaps he was right. Perhaps a doggy gift left on our lawn had been tracked inside and was now stuck to one of our soles. I walked over to the kitchen and examined shoe bottoms. No clues there. On the kitchen counter, I spotted the information sheets sent home by the outpatient surgery center. I scanned down the list of possible catastrophes and found it: "Foul odor."

Although I could not smell it, my son had detected the "foul odor." We were in the six-day wasteland between his surgery and the first post-operative visit. Neither of us had medical training, unless you counted his high school physiology class. Was the smell gangrene? Leading to amputation? Permanent disability? Watching reruns? Eating jelly bagels? On my couch? I rushed to telephone the nurse.

While I was put on hold, I thought of the basketball injury that had brought my son home from college two months earlier than expected. He had gone up for a lay-up and, as he said, smashed into a "bigger guy with a better knee." Jack's knee crunched and dislocated. At the emergency room, the doctor immobilized his knee with a brace, and we received the dreaded late-night call. My husband and I drove down and carried our boy, our 6' 5" college freshman, back home in the back seat of our wagon. Returning to college was not an option. He couldn't climb up into his bunk bed, navigate his way around the sprawling campus, or even tie his shoes. After an MRI revealed torn ligaments and a floating bone chip, along with that wildly skewed kneecap, he decided to withdraw from college and opt for the surgery as soon as possible.

At home, we waited for the swelling to go down before surgery, and I was his nurse, bringing ice packs, water, Tylenol, and Cheetos on demand. For three weeks, he had lived on our couch watching *Love Boat* and *MacGyver*. It was good to feel needed again, but this painful ordeal was need squared. Instead of a sick toddler who needed help getting around, I was dealing with a 240-pound college freshman who was angry at having lost his newfound independence, as was I, come to think of it. I thought all this as I glanced around the corner and saw his body making a new and permanent dent in our brushed leather sofa and saw the red jelly blob on the hardwood floor. Our weekly food bill had doubled, in great part to the giant jar of red vines licorice that sat on our dining room table, the dozen bags of Cheetos, and the many trips for fast food. (With all the fetching, who had time to cook?)

Surrounding him, spreading out into every corner of our home, as his toys had in days past, were his college things: books, notebooks, clothes, video games, CDs, and toiletries. Despite all the disruption, I was enjoying his company until the odd smell manifested under the thick bandages.

At last, the nurse came on the line. I explained my concerns to her in hushed tones so as not to alarm Jack.

"What did the bandage look like when you changed it?" she asked.

"I didn't change it. The instruction sheet said to wait until our first visit," I answered.

"For heaven's sake," she said, but agreed to see the "young prince," as she called him. I shut the windows, locked up the house, and helped him out to the car. He grabbed the car roof and hoisted himself into the backseat, wedging his injured, straight leg out in front in a gymnastic maneuver that could have qualified him for the Cirque de Soleil.

"Couldn't we have waited until *MacGyver* was over?" he asked as we drove along. At the doctor's office, the nurse led us to the casting table and had Jack lie down. His feet hung off the table's end by at least six inches. She began removing the bandages, and I crossed my fingers and waited for the bad news. The smelly, massive infection, or worse, was about to be unveiled. When she finished, all I saw was a neat, maroon wound area.

"Looks great," she said. Not exactly how I'd describe it. Jack propped up on his elbows.

"But what about the smell? It smelled weird earlier," he said.

"I don't smell anything, honey," she reassured him. "This knee is fine." I was relieved to hear that my son was mending nicely and would soon (well, in 12 weeks or so) join the able-bodied once again. And in a few months, he would return to college. Then, the TV would remain silent, and I would no doubt pine for him every time I looked into our living room, saw the permanent dent in the sofa arm or the golden Cheetos dust that lingered behind in the cracks between the pillows. I knew what I would miss most was the sweet sound of his laughter.

Later, back at home, as we pulled into our driveway, I heard an exaggerated "pew—eee" coming from the back seat of my car.

"What is it now?" I asked. "It's not your knee, alright?" I got Jack's crutches, and he hoisted himself out of the car, balanced on the crutches. Glancing over at my neighbor's lawn, I noticed the gardener just finishing his work for the day. He picked up the empty plastic fertilizer bags to throw in the trash. I pointed this out to Jack.

"Cow manure," he said. "Pew—eee!" And we both laughed.

THE OBJECT OF OUR AFFECTION

California, 2006

After the death of our beloved Chihuahua, our family found ourselves pet-less for the first time in years. Still grieving, we all felt it was too soon to get another dog, yet we missed the little guy. Without "Chi," I had a handy excuse to skip my daily walk. My husband missed having the dog in his lap as second-in-command on the remote controller. And our son Jack had taken to luring "stray" cats in through the back door. It was time to act. We needed something to take care of besides ourselves, something to nurture.

Flowers might work, at least temporarily. I set off for the nursery to buy seedlings to plant in pots. Jack came along to carry the large bag of potting soil, or so I thought. While browsing the marigolds and petunias, he slipped away. I found him at the checkout counter, deep in conversation with a nurseryman and cradling a small plant.

"How often do I water it?" he asked. When had he taken such an interest in plants? But it wasn't just any plant. It was a Venus flytrap, the carnivorous plant that traps and eats insects. The perfect blend of pet and freak. We bought the plant.

Back at home, Jack hovered over the Venus flytrap like a father over a new baby. Every morning, he moved the plant to the back yard and measured distilled water into the saucer under the pot. He studied the exact location on the lawn where flies might land. I was brought out for a second opinion, and finally, we found a damp spot where tiny gnats sometimes gathered. He left his new darling outdoors all day until dusk, when he brought it in from the chill. Several days passed without "Venus" catching any prey. Her leaves were wide open like a butterfly's wings. Concerned, Jack decided to transplant his baby into a larger pot. With my vast horticulture knowledge, I was to perform the operation.

The next morning found us in the garden shed perusing spare pots and potting soils. He dragged out a big bag of soil and left me to do the dirty work while he went to the internet to learn more about our new plant. It didn't take long to move the plant into a larger pot with dark, loamy soil. I was watering it from the garden hose when I heard Jack's voice.

"Have you done it yet? I just found out that's not the right type of soil. Did you use the distilled water?"

"Oops," I said.

"You've killed it, you plant assassin," he said.

"Here, you deal with it," I said, handing him the plant.

"Plant assassin," he muttered as I went back inside. I turned around to see a big grin on his face, and we both laughed. After he had set the plant down to recuperate from its close call with eternity, we returned to the nursery to buy the right soil type. Jack discussed pH balances with the nurseryman.

"It's sphagnum moss, and it has to be in the range of 4.0 to 4.5," Jack insisted. I hadn't seen him this interested in science since his sixth-grade hooked-on-hydraulics project. As he and the nurseryman talked dirt, I reflected on our Venus flytrap. This delicate-looking carnivorous plant had somehow managed to become our replacement pet.

Sure, we couldn't cuddle with it, but it had distinct advantages over a Chihuahua. Like the Parisians who carry their dogs everywhere, we too could now take our pet to grocery stores and even restaurants. At our favorite outdoor cafe, "Venus" might even come in handy, considering the flies that sometimes appeared plate side begging for food. There would be no exorbitant vet bills or marked furniture.

When we got home, Jack opened the bag of moss. I removed the "wrong" dirt, replaced it with the correct type, and carefully patted down the soil around the plant's thin stem. While I held the pot in my hands, Jack poured a slight stream of distilled water into the saucer where the pot would rest. Seeing my son gently place our "Venus" onto the saucer, I felt satisfied. The plant somehow looked healthier, thanks to our joint efforts. I stared at its delicate, slightly rose-colored inner leaves and felt something warm and familiar in my chest. A tenderness, I realized, the kind that comes from nurturing someone, or something other than yourself. Our 2½-inch new pet hadn't caught a single insect, yet it had successfully captured us.

MIGHTY APHRODITE

California, 2007

Everyone needs a friend who is larger than life; the strong, silent type who is a good listener. And if she happens to be much older and has a sketchy past, so much the better. In Malibu, California, I found just such a friend who was always there for me.

My friend Aphrodite arrived in California in the late 1980s to make her home at the Getty Museum. I first encountered her ringed by admirers who gazed at the strong lines of her 7½-foot frame. She stood on her pedestal, proud and sure of herself, holding court. Being in the limelight was easy for her since she had spent a number of years underground.

The 2,400-year-old Aphrodite was brought to the Getty to be the centerpiece of its antiquities collection. The museum paid $18 million for her. And to think, she has a chipped nose and is bald—although she probably originally had hair and a veil.

Over the two decades, I visited her more than a dozen times, awed every time by her immense size. Her voluptuousness is stunning and quite reassuring. It's nice to know that plus-size women were valued at some point in history, and in her case, she was known as the most beautiful goddess, goddess of love and queen of the heavens.

The information placard claimed her size is what makes her a goddess. If big equals good, does that make me and my fellow size-14 women goddesses, too? I would like to think so.

What I like best is that she looks strong. Being that powerful, I imagine she didn't have to put up with too many antics from her husbands and lovers.

Being married to that ugly Hephaestus, the god of fire, must have been difficult for someone so lovely, but she never complained. If I could get her to talk, I'd offer her a shoulder to cry on—although she might crush me in the process.

The placard placed near her base says that the wind-blown garments clinging to her body are characteristic of Aphrodite, goddess of love.

But I know the truth: The real reason she's dressed in a loose toga is to downplay those thunderous thighs. The woman is smart—she knows she wouldn't look good in a miniskirt.

She's a hardheaded woman. Marble, to be precise. Her head looks a little small for her limestone body. Some have speculated that her current head might not be her head at all. She could be a composite of two ancient artworks.

Whatever the case, having a head that is, well, completely different from your body is tough. Talk about feeling disconnected.

And as if this head thing weren't enough, her origins are in question. She could be from North Africa or Sicily. Sicily is more likely, since the limestone she's made of is of the Sicilian type, according to the geologists at the University of Palermo in Italy. Experts at the Getty also believe that the limestone is closest to the Sicilian variety.

I don't know why anyone had to consult the scientists to figure out she is Sicilian. All they had to do was ask me.

After 25 years around a Sicilian mother-in-law, I can assure you Aphrodite is a Sicilian girl. She's larger than life and exudes power from every square inch of her body and face. One look at those serious eyes, and you know not to mess with her.

Need more proof that she's Sicilian? Take a look at her outstretched arm and open hand. It's obvious the woman is begging for a snack. It could have been a golden apple or a pomegranate that she wanted, but I'm sure it was a large slice of pizza.

For the moment, she seems comfortable at the Getty Villa in Malibu, but she will soon be moving home because Italy wants her back.

Italy, Malibu, either will work as long as the big girl stays near the sea. After all, she was born of the sea and had many temples built by the sea, so she probably feels most at home by the coast, surrounded by admirers.

I must admit I'm a little envious of my friend Aphrodite. To be mostly bald, plus size, oh-so-old, and to have so many folks fighting over you—now that's heaven.

ARRIVEDERCI, MY GOOD FRIEND

California, 2010

A few years later, my larger-than-life friend left Malibu quietly, escorted by Italian police officers, to take a plane back to Rome en route to her native Sicily. When I wrote about her in August of 2007 for the *Christian Science Monitor* (Home Forum section), I admired her for being a plus-size woman, 1,300 pounds, seven-plus feet tall, and much admired by art lovers who ringed her as she stood on display at the Getty Villa. I was also envious that despite being so very old, at 2,400 years, ancient in fact, folks fought over her. The Italians said she was illegally removed from their soil, and the Getty Museum wanted to keep her. It was this custody battle that ultimately caused Aphrodite to be dismantled one December and sent packing back to Sicily.

A book released in 2011, *Chasing Aphrodite: The Hunt for Looted Antiquities at the World's Richest Museum* by Ralph Frammolino (published by Houghton Mifflin Harcourt), describes the fight over Aphrodite between the Getty Museum, which has kept her since the late 1980s, and the Italians who wanted their big girl back on home soil. Two pieces of evidence led to her leaving Malibu: photographs and ties to the underworld—and not the type usually associated with gods such as Hades, or the goddess Persephone. Photos discovered in 2006 by Getty-hired detectives showed poor Aphrodite at her worst, scattered about in fragments lying in dirt and with grime covering her lovely face. The investigators say her former owner was a friend of an alleged Sicilian antiquities smuggler who had ties to the mafia. When told of the evidence of Aphrodite's shady past, and seeing the photos, the Getty agreed to return their beloved goddess to the Italian authorities.

Her checkered past and the mystique that surrounds her make her all the more endearing to her admirers and especially to me. She is a survivor who has endured being buried underground, broken into fragments, and being spirited away to a foreign country against her will. Aphrodite is a strong Sicilian woman, and now she has arrived in Aidone, Sicily near Morgantina where she was buried for centuries before coming to the US. Upon her arrival in Sicily, she was greeted by crowds, not surprisingly.

Even though I might not get to visit her again, I wish her well. I hope she will soon be back on her pedestal, working the crowds, enjoying the attention she so deserves. After all, not only is she the queen of heaven and the goddess of love, but the old girl still rocks.

UNE TASSE DE THÉ

France, 2006

After two weeks in France, I found myself counting the days till we would fly back to the States. Although I was enjoying my spring trip with my traveling companion and older son, Anthony, I was starting to miss my husband and younger son who had stayed back in California for work and school. Anthony indulged me throughout our trip by seeking out the nearest internet café in each town we visited, so I could stay in touch with my guys back home.

Upon our arrival in Aix-en-Provence, we found an internet café which also happened to be the local watering hole. Every day, we stopped by the café and sat at separate computer terminals to check our emails and write to family and friends. One afternoon after reading a romantic email from my husband, I felt more homesick than ever. I wrote back and then logged off the computer to tell Anthony I was ready to leave the smoke-filled café and go find some supper. I saw him at the bar drinking beer and conversing with another gentleman in rapid-fire French. Although I speak a little French, I could only understand the occasional word. Since there were no empty seats near my son, I found a spot at the end of the bar by the door with cleaner air and a view of the busy, cobble-stoned street. The bartender, friendly and patient with my limited French, took my order.

"Une tasse de thé, s'il vous plaît ?" I asked in broken French. He promptly served up a tiny pot of hot water and a cup with a teabag. As he served me, he said something that sounded likc, "Another lady orders tea. An American." I nodded and smiled, acting like I understood. I slowly sipped the fragrant brew, and he left to serve other patrons. Glancing out the door, I watched people scurrying up and down the street—couples and families out enjoying the late afternoon. How fun it would be to walk arm-in-arm with my husband down the old streets of Aix, past cafes and cathedrals, taking in the sights. I missed him. Instead of feeling homesick, I cupped my hand around the warm cup and tried to savor my tea.

The waning afternoon light turned into evening, and I felt the pensiveness brought on by the "L'heure bleue." The bartender refilled the tiny pot with hot water, and as I tried to coax the tired teabag back to life, I had an idea where the expression "down in the cups" had originated. With a sea of foreign voices all around and my son preoccupied with his new acquaintance, I had never felt so alone.

"Voila!" The bartender spoke. I looked up from my tea to see the friendly face of a woman, about my age, with salt and pepper hair. It was the American he had spoken of earlier. She offered her hand and introduced herself as Habiba. Along with her daughter, Habiba was living in Aix while doing research at the local university. Although she had been born in Algeria, she had lived and worked in the States for many years. And best of all, she was from Atlanta!

She ordered her tea and sat down next to me while her daughter used the internet. We quickly settled into a comfortable conversation—in rapid-fire English—discussing our families, motherhood, the South, and everything else in between. The time passed quickly as I listened to her lilting accent and felt suddenly very much at home in the fading twilight.

An hour or so later, when it was time to leave, we exchanged emails and promised to keep in touch. And we did. When I returned to the States, we emailed to one another and deepened our friendship for the next several months. When she wrote to tell me she would be in California for the holidays, we decided to get together for brunch.

On the appointed day, the first thing I saw when she and her husband pulled up was her smiling face. She climbed out, and we hugged. I felt I had known her for years. She handed me a gift bag.

I can't say I was surprised by what I found inside the bag. A cheerful tin of designer tea bags—green tea with cherry blossoms. As our families visited and got to know each other further, Habiba and I picked up our conversation right where we'd left off at the internet café in Provence. We spoke of work, children, health, and hopes. Soon, I told her, we were going to move to the Georgia countryside, just a few hours north of her. Knowing such a wonderful, new friend would be nearby was a big comfort to me and gave me confidence about our upcoming move.

"I can't believe we had to travel halfway around the world to meet each other," Habiba said, squeezing my hand. Brought together by fate, I thought, or a simple cup of tea.

SPRING RITUAL

Pennsylvania, 2006

One Easter I found myself far from home, a guest in a house weighed down with sorrow. A few days earlier we had traveled from California to the hills of western Pennsylvania to bury my father-in-law.

Behind closed doors downstairs, my husband slept or grieved, or possibly both. In the kitchen on this gloomy morning, my mother-in-law bravely tried to get back to the business of living. She stood at the window, chopping carrots, celery, and potatoes for a stew. Nearby, my nine-year-old niece, Marie, and I played with dolls. Chewing on a strand of her long dark hair, she told me each doll's name and showed me their interchangeable outfits. One of them had beautiful long black hair, like her late mother, like Marie herself. I told her so. She looked pleased. Suddenly, my mother-in-law yelled.

"Quick, grab a towel or a flyswatter! It's a quarter till noon."

"Why?" I asked, but jumped into motion, opened the kitchen drawer to pull out dry, clean towels. "Is there a fly somewhere?"

"Open all the windows," she directed. As I cranked open the window, she explained that in just a few minutes, she would carry out a Sicilian custom, a family tradition she had practiced for more than seven decades. At noon, on the day Jesus rose from the tomb on the Saturday before Easter, the women stopped their work to chase out the devil. Her Sicilian mother had brought the custom to America when she immigrated in the 1920s, using brooms or sticks to beat the walls and force the devil out the window. Since the house we were in was newer, and the home of her son-in-law, my mother-in-law improvised with towels and a flyswatter. She invited me to join her but didn't pressure me.

I told her I'd participate. Almost anything was an improvement on the heaviness that bore down on all of us. My niece motioned me to follow her upstairs. We ran in and out of various rooms, rapidly cranking open windows. Marie laughed and called out to me, reporting her progress.

"I got my room, you get Grandma's," she said.

"What about the closets?" I asked.

"Yes, open them," she answered, her voice rising in excitement as the hour neared. After we finished upstairs, we rushed to the basement, but not before my mother-in-law cautioned me, "Don't open the windows down there. The spiders will get in."

Couldn't the devil be in the basement? I wondered. And if so, how would he leave? Were the spiders a more tangible threat on this day? And there was the question of whether to disturb my husband, still silent behind closed doors. I don't think the devil would want to tangle with my husband first thing in the morning. I know I don't. I decided to leave him be.

Tools in hand—Marie and I with dish towels, my mother-in-law with a fly swatter—we waited under the kitchen clock. The vegetables simmered on the stove, and the steam drifted up to the ceiling. My mother-in-law told us what to say as we performed the spring ritual.

"Devil be gone, levati di cca diavulu," she said. "Repeat this as you run through the rooms waving the dish towels. I'll get this area with the fly swatter."

"It's time," Marie shouted, pointing to the clock's straight-up hands. We took off and darted through the rooms of the house like hellions, waving and flapping towels.

"Devil be gone, devil be gone," and "levati di cca diavulu," we chanted. The swoosh of the fly swatter and the crisp snap of towels accompanied our chorus. After 10 minutes or so, Marie and I reunited in the kitchen. We were breathing hard with faces pink from all the running and shouting. Marie laughed, and I felt exhilarated.

My mother-in-law opened a bottle of holy water and sprinkled the walls. "To bring God into the house," she explained. Marie and I stood quietly, observing.

Through the open window, I saw the white blossoms of an apple tree resting upon an expanse of emerald lawn. The clean spring air drifted in, filling the dark and heavy spaces left behind by the sadness of the past week. The air felt light, our moods were lifted. I am not sure whether we had succeeded in ridding the house of the devil, but it didn't seem to matter. We were ready for a new season. We were full of life.

RETURNING TO AGRIGENTO'S GREEK TEMPLES

Sicily, 2009

In the summer of 2000, my first visit to the ancient temples in Agrigento, Sicily, was to the tune of pop music. Claudio Baglioni, an Italian version of Tom Jones, had set up shop at the temples' site. Our guide tried unsuccessfully to compete with his crooning and the thunderous music that echoed around the ruins. I hoped one day my family and I would one day have a quieter, more pensive visit to this World Heritage landmark.

Nine years later I returned there with my family. From our hotel below the Valley of the Temples, I took in the view I remembered from before. Against a clear sky stood the temple ruins, more than 2000 years old. Some are now just a collection of broken columns, but the Temple Concordia stands proudly intact, its columns orange-tinted in the afternoon sun.

The second day of our visit, we met up with our guide from before, Giovanna, an Agrigento native who grew up playing in the Valley of the Temples. She led us through the temples' park telling us about the history and culture of this place. With no pop music to distract, and Giovanna's perfect English, we learned that the rectangular shape of the temples and columns suggests the Greek, patriarchal culture. We stopped in the ruins of the temple Tempio di Ercole (Temple of Hercules), who back in the day was the national hero of both Agrigento and Sicily, their version of Superman. Standing between the 32-foot-tall columns and looking down below at fields and the Mediterranean, it was easy to see how foreigners arriving by sea might have been intimidated by the power and wealth these temples represented.

Founded in 589 B.C., Agrigento was known as Akragas and was at one time the richest city in the Mediterranean, a trade center. Today, Agrigento is not so wealthy as it was then, but the temples that once intimidated potential invaders now lure tourists from all over the world.

Along with dozens of sightseers, we walked by groves of almond and olive trees, stopping to view the Temples

Concordia and Juno. At the stadium-sized Temple of Zeus, a 25-foot-tall stone telamone figure lies among the ruins looking like a humongous sunbather. This stone giant represented Atlas, who supported the world on his shoulders.

All these giants and supermen left me pondering the lives of ordinary folk.

"What would life have been like for women in the days these temples were used for worship?" I asked our guide.

"You could have been a wife, and never gotten to go out much except to worship. Or a mistress, or a prostitute." None of these roles sounded appealing. Back then, life must have been bleak if you happened to be born female. Giovanna asked if we would like to see the Temple of Castor and Pollux. I was beginning to feel I'd seen enough of these big columns—until she elaborated.

"Next to the Temple of Castor and Pollux are a pair of altars used in the worship of Demeter and Persephone," she said. Now she had caught my attention. Demeter was the goddess responsible for agriculture in Sicily, or so the ancients thought. And I have always been fascinated with Demeter and her daughter Persephone.

"I'd like to see it," I told Giovanna. I followed her to a less crowded, quieter area, not as well-preserved as some of the rest of the temples.

Out of the shadows of the tall columns, we approached an area of flat stones laid out in a circular pattern. This rounded arrangement evoked a softer, comforting mood. Our guide invited us to take a seat on the stone "benches" and told us about the yearly festival where only women were allowed.

In the fifth century B.C., married women gathered at this place to honor Demeter, the goddess of fertility and patroness of marriage. In this ancient version of a three-day slumber party, the women danced and ate special foods. On one of the days, they fasted and cursed at one another. A round altar with a hollowed-out area was used for offerings of live piglets and snake or phallic-shaped breads. A nearby square altar used for sacrificing animals bears a reddish tint, the mark of ancient fires. Later, the women would retrieve the remains of the sacrifices and mix them with seeds to ensure a plentiful crop.

As I sat in the same spot where my sisters of long ago also sat, I relaxed into the warmth cast off by the stone bench beneath me. I imagined their happy time away from their men and daily lives. Running my hand along the ancient stone seat, in the quietness of this place, I could almost hear their laughter.

I wish I could have been there to party along with them. I would have loved the dancing and the special food, but I'm not too good at fasting. I'd be cursing too if I hadn't eaten all day. Then again, if I got too hungry, I would have had to sneak off behind an olive tree and sample one of those funny-shaped loaves of bread. I can almost taste it!

LESSONS FROM VAN GOGH

France, 2006

As a writer who depends on the whims of the muse, I traveled to the south of France one spring to find out what had inspired my favorite artist, Vincent van Gogh, during his most productive period. On a self-guided tour around St. Remy-de-Provence called "Sur Les Pas de Vincent van Gogh" (in the footsteps of van Gogh) I meandered along the same paths where van Gogh walked and painted more than a century ago. There I saw provincial landscapes filled with light and color, felt a teasing wind that he captured in many of his paintings. Standing under the hot May sun amidst olive groves, fields and flowers, I contemplated this remarkable man and his difficult life.

Like many creative people, van Gogh faced challenges such as an eccentric personality, mental problems, and a lack of emotional support for his endeavors. Yet, despite these overwhelming obstacles, van Gogh pursued his passion and produced an astonishing 1050 drawings and some 870 paintings during his short life of 37 years. How, I wondered, was he able to accomplish so much?

He was consumed in his own creativity, often immersed in his own work, and sometimes in a bottle. Like many writers, artists, and actors, he faced a lack of support, emotional and financial, for his work. His odd behavior (he was probably bipolar and also afflicted with seizures) and irritating personality (a terrible lack of social skills) made sustaining friends difficult. Van Gogh turned to his brother Theo for support. Theo gave him a stipend of 200 francs a month, not a small sum in the 1880s, and corresponded frequently with his brother. With few flesh-and-bones friends around him, van Gogh cherished these letters. He wrote back to Theo, sharing ideas on technique and subjects, and enthusiastically outlined his plans for his many art projects.

In St. Remy-de-Provence, I walked through St. Paul's Mental Hospital, where van Gogh spent a full year toward the end of his life. There, doctors and the staff recognized and fostered his talent. They gave him a room with a huge window overlooking a colorful palette of gardens and fields, and a second room to use as his studio. During his stay there, while undergoing treatment for his mental problems, van Gogh produced 150 paintings and more than 100 drawings. In this supportive environment, van Gogh experienced one of the most productive periods of his life and created "The Irises," "Starry Night," "Olive Grove in the Evening," "Field of Wheat with Cypress Tree," and "Reaper in a Wheat Field."

Van Gogh scared people with his eccentric behavior—temperamental outbursts, seizures, and heavy drinking, to name a few. On one occasion, he tried to stab his friend Gaugin but failed. Later, he cut off part of his own ear and presented it to the women at the local brothel as "something to remember me by." With antics like these, and not surprisingly, van Gogh had trouble finding models willing to pose for him. He improvised, working with what was available. The result? A portrait of a doctor, a café owner, scenes of his own bedroom and the courtyard at the mental hospital, and numerous landscapes near where he lived. Featured in his paintings are olive groves, vineyards, cypress trees, and the chalky-topped mountain range of Les Alpilles.

Van Gogh believed in his art even when few others did. Although he had the support of his brother Theo, and was nurtured during his stay at the mental hospital in St. Remy, most people did not care for his paintings because they were unconventional. In fact, he sold only one painting in his lifetime, "The Red Vineyard," although he traded some of his art for meals. Despite his roller coaster moods, seizures, and bouts drinking absinthe, van Gogh plunged forward in his work and painted most days.

Unlike van Gogh's Theo, my brother never offered to support me financially. And although my writing sometimes makes me crazy, I haven't yet had to check into an institution. Sometimes, finding even an hour away from the noisy hubbub of daily life is almost impossible, but I have found "riches" in other places. Friends and other creative souls act as my sounding board, as Theo was for Vincent. They have cheered me on through the inevitable lows of writing, such as less productive periods and the inevitable rejection slips that come with the territory.

Every time I receive a rejection and feel the sting of self-doubt, I think of van Gogh. After all, I have sold much of my work, as compared to van Gogh's one painting. Why should I let one little rejection stand in the way of my progress?

Although van Gogh ultimately took his own life, it is not this tragedy that I chose to think about as I left the hospital grounds and continued my journey in van Gogh's footsteps. As I moved through the countryside in the afternoon sun, I reflected upon this man who fought his own inner battles while creating colorful, light-filled masterpieces, this artist who followed his passions despite what the world thought of him. I thought of the man behind the brilliant brushstrokes who had found a way to practice his art in spite of so many obstacles, and I was awed. On the horizon, a light wind brushed against the olive trees, and van Gogh's legacy spoke.

Listen to your inner voice. Do the work you must. Let your passion drive you.

OTHER PUBLISHED WORKS

CREATIVE NONFICTION

Art Lessons (*Chicken Soup for the Soul: Messages from Heaven*, 2012)

Outrageous Okra (*Stories to Warm a Grandma's Heart*, 2011)

Memories of Jackson's Elegant and Inviting Carmichael House (*Georgia Backroads*, Winter 2009)

Aphrodite's Mighty Appeal (*Christian Science Monitor*, August 2007)

Spring Cleaning (*Chicken Soup for the Soul: All in the Family*, 2009)

Une Tasse de Thé (*Chicken Soup for the Tea Lover's Soul*, 2012)

Frosty Georgia Morning (*Chicken Soup for the Horse Lover's Soul*, 2003)

Southern Spirit (*Chicken Soup for the Horse Lover's Soul II*, 2006)

Object of Our Affection (*The Ultimate Gardener*, 2009)

Southernspeak (*Georgia Backroads*, Winter 2008)

Grandma's Okra (*Georgia Backroads*, Fall 2008)

Empty Nest Refilled (as found on boomerwomenspeak.com, 2003)

Outrageous Okra (*Guideposts Magazine*, September 2006)

Fall Ritual (*Georgia Backroads*, Fall 2006)

Van Gogh's Canvas (Palisades Post, March 29, 2007*)*

Georgia Five (Georgia Backroads, Autumn 2010*)*

Picture Hat (Project Keepsake anthology, Native Ink Press, 2014*)*

A Neighbor's Gift (Telling Stories, Calhoun Area Writers, 2019*)*

"Boomerang" Column (*Catoosa Life Magazine*, 2007-2016)

Legacy of Storytelling (Georgia Magazine, 2015*)*

PUBLISHED FICTION

Moon Over Taylor's Ridge

Published 2012, Little Creek Books, Johnson City, TN

Return to Taylor's Crossing

Published 2015, Janie Dempsey Watts

Mothers, Sons, Beloveds, and Other Strangers

Published 2017, Bold Horses Press

CHILDREN'S BOOK

Pap Pap Goes to Paris, and so does Ricky

Published May 3, 2018, Janie Dempsey Watts

ACKNOWLEDGMENTS

Many people have helped make this book possible in different ways. Thanks to Jimmy Espy for giving me my own column, "Boomerang," and to my editor, Victor Miller, who gave me free rein. And a shoutout to the editors at *Chicken Soup for the Soul* books, *Guideposts*, *The Christian Science Monitor*, *Georgia Backroads*, *Georgia Magazine,* and *Palisades Post* who published my stories. A huge thanks to my first readers of this book, Ellen Young McCashin, Kathe Traynham, and the talented author Amber Lanier Nagle. Amber also steered this project through design and production. She offered to write a description for my book cover. I can never thank her enough for her encouragement and support.

A special thanks to two much-admired authors, Renea Winchester and Barbara Tucker. Both took time to read my manuscript and offer their impressions for the back cover.

These tales could not have been written without those people who shared their stories with me. These include Verna Bible, Brett Jones, Jeanette Wilbanks, Wayne Childers, and to those now in heaven, Barbara Watts, Mildred Capehart, Shannon Capehart, and the Dunn sisters. And as always, gratitude to the mayor of Woodstation, Sue Gracy, who knows all the local history. I appreciate those with whom I shared adventures, Anne Turley, my big brother Dean Watts, my sister Emily Watts Card, and my late sister, Judy Watts, who was the best horse helper ever. Thank you to my best friend Ellen Young McCashin for her unfailing support. And to others who were there on the journey, Nancy Martin, Giovanna Lombardo, Habiba Deming, Dr. Michael White, Jim and Dorcus McBrayer, and my late family members Frances Spataro, Waymond Watts, and Chuck Martin. To anyone who was part of these tales, whether behind the scenes or mentioned in these stories, thank you. My special thanks to my sons, Anthony and Jack, and to my husband, Stephen, who shares my love of nature, horses, and the farm.

These stories could not have been written without the inspiration of my late parents, Anne Dempsey Watts and Ray Dean Watts, and my late grandmothers, Avie Ann Williams

Watts, and Bertha Carmichael Dempsey. I am forever grateful.

ABOUT THE AUTHOR

A native of Chattanooga, Tennessee, Janie Dempsey Watts has family roots in north Georgia, where her grandparents lived on the family farm. Her childhood experiences with her family on the farm fueled her imagination and her desire to write. She left the South and moved to California to study journalism at the University of California, Berkeley (B.A.) and the University of Southern California (M.A.) After her children were raised, she and her husband returned to the South and now live near her family farm not far from Taylor's Ridge.

Her non-fiction and fiction works have been extensively published in newspapers, magazines, anthologies, and literary journals. She is the author of two novels (*Moon Over Taylor's Ridge* and *Return to Taylor's Crossing*), a short story collection (*Mothers, Sons, Beloveds, and Other Strangers*), and a picture book, *Pap Pap Goes to Paris, and so does Ricky.*

Please visit her at www.janiewatts.com to learn more about her award-winning books.

www.ingramcontent.com/pod-product-compliance
Lightning Source LLC
LaVergne TN
LVHW100512110826
845146LV00002B/613

* 9 7 9 8 2 1 8 8 3 8 4 6 1 *